MONTANA'S COWBOYS
LIVING THE HERITAGE

BY DANIEL N. VICHOREK

MONTANA GEOGRAPHIC SERIES

NUMBER 20

MONTANA MAGAZINE

AMERICAN & WORLD GEOGRAPHIC PUBLISHING

LARRY MAYER/BILLINGS GAZETTE

Dedication

This book is dedicated to my father, Victor D. Vichorek, 1910-1981. Upon his death he behind the following:

- 1 custom-built saddle with tack
- 1 saddle carbine, model 1894, with scabbard
- 1 six-shooter with shells corroded green in cylinder
- 1 clean Stetson for going to town
- 1 sweat-soaked Stetson for work
- 1 pair unfaded Levis for going to town
- 1 pair faded Levis for work
- 1 pair worn-out Levis
- 1 pair riding boots
- 1 pair dress boots, circa 1940, shiny black with four rows of white-leather diamo running up the tops
- and some other stuff that we took to the dump, where it was overdue.

He tried to teach his sons to ride, to shoot, and to always speak the truth. Sorry, Pap, got one out of three.

Library of Congress Cataloging-in-Publication Data

Vichorek, Daniel N.
  Montana's cowboys : living the heritage / by Daniel N. Vichorek.
  Includes index.
  ISBN 1-56037-066-1
  1. Cowboys--Montana--Interviews. 2. Ranch life--Montana. 3. Montana-
-Social life and customs. I. Montana magazine. II. Title. III. Series.
F735.V63 1994
978.6--dc20   94-18971

Write for our catalog:
American & World Geographic Publishing, P.O. Box 5630, Helena, MT 59604.
Printed in U.S.A. by Fenske Companies, Billings, Montana

Contents

Left: J.W. Roberts.
Facing page, left: Tools of the rodeo trade.
Bottom: And make no mistake about it.
Title page: Cowboy clothes? Hard-workin' clothes. WILL BREWSTER
Front cover: There's always coffee. SOC CLAY
Back cover, top: Horse roundup. LARRY MAYER/BILLINGS GAZETTE
Left: Calf roper's gear. BOB ZELLAR/J-R AGENCY
Right: After the ride at the Dillon rodeo. LARRY MAYER/BILLINGS GAZETTE

LARRY MAYER/BILLINGS GAZETTE

Thanks

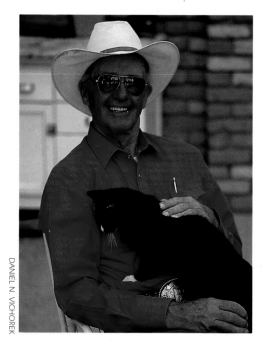

DANIEL N. VICHOREK

Above: Sonny Linger and friend.

Facing page: Big sky, big cattle.

LARRY MAYER/BILLINGS GAZETTE

This is to thank everybody named in this book, and the others who helped me but aren't in here. You know who you are.

I owe special gratitude to those who offered me food not only for my soul but also for my body. These include Babe Billingsley and Shelley Mackay, who fed me mule deer meat and proved "they're really good if you get a good one." Others who took care of me were the men at the Binion ranch, and the Binion chef, Cyndi Horne, whose delicate touch turned longhorn meat into ambrosia. R.D. Horne cheered me up telling me about his cowboy wedding. John and Mary Hammett fed me cowboy chili and sent me a photograph after they decided the ones I took couldn't possibly come out. My undying appreciation goes to Marty Hedoesit, the happy bear roper, who stayed cheerful no matter how much I bothered him. My gratitude to Leo Plain Feather, wagon boss, manager of great herds, and buffalo wrangler. Thanks to Greg Sevier at the Binion ranch, who explained western hospitality after he had practiced it on me. And my most special gratitude to Ray Krone, who not only fed me real food for real people but inspired me with his knowledge, experience, and vocabulary. And thanks to Sonny Linger, who told me where to find the dinosaur Ray Krone. Jim Salmond, descendant of the Cattle Queen of Montana, was endlessly patient with the greenhorn writer, hauled me around the old stomping grounds, and turned his pickup around 100 times so I could take pictures without getting blown out of the county. Thanks to the world rodeo champ Benny Reynolds for being patient with yet another character who wanted to ask him a lot of damn-fool questions.

Glenn Swank was most helpful in explaining operation of the roundup wagon, and settling my confusion about whether cattle roost in trees or sleep sideways. Ernest Tooke took me to the sacred battleground of his ancestors and showed me the present-day Tooke horses, besides providing invaluable literature in the form of his excellent book, *Moments in Rodeo*. I'm going to read his other book too. Pete Story kindly provided me information about his famous ancestor and the family ranch. After visiting Cal's Custom Boot Shop in Bozeman and The Kirkpatrick Custom Hat Company in Wisdom, I decided I needed a new hat and pair of boots. I visited the Gator Rope Company in Helena, but I don't need a rope. Afraid I'd hurt myself with it.

And thanks to Lory Morrow and Becca Kohl of the Montana Historical Society Photo Archives for their thorough and cheerful assistance.

Thanks, folks. All the screw-ups are mine alone.

Just What Are Cowboys?

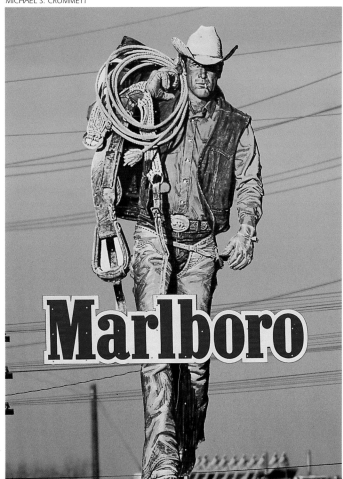

Daryll Dosson, a real cowboy (right), versus the commercial image.

JAMES WOODCOCK

What are cowboys anyway? The earliest use of the word seems to pertain to some anti-revolutionary rabble-rousers who plundered patriots in New York in the time of the Revolutionary War. What they had to do with cows is not certain. Since then, polite society has occasionally used the term in a slighting manner to indicate a certain wildness and irresponsibility. Two presidents of the United States have been referred to as "that damned cowboy." In spy novels and in testimony before Congress, renegade CIA agents and other federal officers who decide to ride roughshod over official policy and run their own show are called "cowboys."

This use of the word "cowboy" was particularly annoying to Sonny Linger, who has long worked with rodeos in various capacities, besides working as a ranch cowboy. Slanders on the cowboy name aside, Linger said, the cowboy image is still strong in America. "People need heroes," he said. In a recent nationwide poll, a third of adults polled said they had a strong interest in the West, and the western life. They said they regarded it as an escape from the pressures of everyday life.

The popularity of the cowboy image explains why it is so effective in selling products. How many Marlboros have been sold to men and women who hoped that a pack of cigarettes would somehow bring them closer to the clean virile world where the Marlboro man seems to live?

This book does not psychoanalyze cowboys or their fans. What it attempts to do instead is to take a look at what remains of the cowboy life in Montana today. Montana, after all, was the destination of thousands of cowboys who set out from Texas with herds of cattle in the 19th century. As the state prepares to enter the 21st century, it probably is high time to see what happened to some of those young men and their way of life.

The question of who is a cowboy remains unanswered. One of the people I interviewed for this book,

Wet day on the range.

DIANE ENSIGN

Ray Krone, says you ain't a cowboy if you ain't got the old skills and knowledge that went with handling cattle and horses on the open range without barns and fences and all the rest. Krone and others said that rodeo performers are not necessarily cowboys in any meaningful way, because a lot of them are just athletes who went to school to learn rodeo. As Krone said, some of them "don't know if a cow roosts in a tree or sleeps on the ground."

Nevertheless, there is a strong contingent of rodeo cowboys who learned their skills on working ranches, and when their rodeo days are over, they ride off to spend their sunset years on their own ranches. Hardly any proficient ranch cowboy has not at one time or another at least thought of getting into the rodeo.

All of the people interviewed for this book make their living in some phase of the cattle business. None of them is a cowboy in the 19th century sense of a person who works seasonally for low wages and then attempts to stay drunk the rest of the year. I do not solve the mystery of when a cowboy becomes a cowman. Some cowboys are eighty years old. I believe a cowboy becomes a cowman when he comes to own at least one cow. Having once been a cowboy, however, he remains one, just adding the new title to show he is not only a lover, a fighter, and a wild bull rider—as the saying goes—but also a capitalist. Even the word "capital" comes originally from the same root word as "cattle" in Latin.

I do not know why there are cowgirls but no cow women. I did talk to two women ranchers, but I wouldn't call them cow women without their permission. One of them goes armed. There is a group of women secure enough to call themselves Cowbelles, but I understand they are an auxiliary of sorts.

Besides examining personalities and events, I have attempted to convey some sense of the environment where cattle are raised, and which was and is such a major element of the cowboy life and image. I attempted to fathom something of the Zen of steer roping, the cowboy's favorite

Above: *Even in this day and age, they're still called cowgirls.*

Facing page: *A wagon full of old and new.*

I believe a cowboy becomes a cowman when he comes to own at least one cow.

JEFF & ALEXA HENRY

sport, and learned that the joy of it compares to that found by others in shopping and fly fishing. We even catch a glimpse of one of the real Marlboro Men, gone somewhat to seed.

I have tried to show something of the early history by recounting the 1866 cattle drive from Texas by Nelson Story, the original real-life person behind the story *Lonesome Dove,* of which we know too little. The Cattle Queen of Montana also appears here. I talked with one of her descendants and visited her old ranch. She was once portrayed in the movies by Barbara Stanwyck, which shows how important she was.

This is the age of debunking. What this means is that college professors and other authorities investigate the basis of everything we have ever held sacred and then announce that it was a fake. Cowboys have come in for their share of debunking.

Wallace Stegner, college professor, Pulitzer Prize-winning author and authority on all things western, had this to say about cowboys: "The cowboy in practice was and is an overworked, underpaid hireling, almost as homeless and dispossessed as a modern crop worker, and his fabled independence was and is chiefly the privilege of quitting his job in order to go looking for another just as bad."

William Forbis, another professor and author of the Time-Life book *The Cowboys*, said the cowboy was "A sweaty little man, tall in the saddle." Further, he wrote, "The American cowboy was actually a dirty, overworked laborer who fried his brains under a prairie sun, or rode endless miles in rain and wind to mend fences or look for lost calves." Evidently it was a hell of a life all right, and we're well off to be rid of it.

I certainly have not attempted to write anything approaching a comprehensive history of the cow business, cowboys, or anything else. Many excellent, easy-to-find books have gone in that direction.

BERT GILDART

DIANE ENSIGN

Above: Proper attire at the Miles City Bucking Horse Sale.

Facing page: Cowboys and farmers don't mix.

DIANE ENSIGN

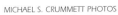

MICHAEL S. CRUMMETT PHOTOS

Above: It's a lifestyle, right down to the slogans on your rig.
Right: Frying Rocky Mountain oysters.

Facing page: Leading the string.

Nelson Story and the Original Montana Cowboys

L.A. HUFFMAN PHOTO, MONTANA HISTORICAL SOCIETY

History does not tell us much about the first cowboys in Montana. We're not even sure who they were, but chances are they were the men that Nelson Story brought up from Texas with the first trail herd in 1866. In that case, most of the first Montana cowboys were ex-Confederate soldiers, recruited in destitute post-war Texas.

Let the tale be told from the beginning.

Nelson Story was born in the hillbilly country of southeastern Ohio in 1838. When he was 16, he left for the frontier, possibly because of some whittling he may have performed on his girlfriend's brother.

He turned up at Leavenworth, Kansas, freighting from there to Denver. Denver at the time was a small collection of miners' shacks, saloons and bordellos. Colorado apparently had some promise, and Story took up silver mining there. In 1863 he lit out for Alder Gulch in Montana. He reportedly had a good claim in the gulch above Virginia City, and also made money freighting. When the vigilance committee was formed in 1863, Story was there; he was one of the original signers of the vigilante oath. Some accounts say he helped with at least one of the vigilante hangings, possibly kicking the box from under the doomed man himself.

In the spring of 1866, Story took $30,000 worth of gold, close to 140 pounds, to New York, where he exchanged it for $40,000 in greenbacks. He sewed $10,000 of this into his clothes and headed for Texas.

Nelson Story's great-grandson, Pete Story, says his ancestor left no record of what he was planning. The record shows that Nelson spent the early summer buying cattle and hiring cowboys in the vicinity of Fort Worth. Accounts differ as to the number purchased; Pete Story sets the number at about a thousand: bulls, steers, and cows, some with calves.

In 1866, it was a buyers' market for both cattle and cowboys in Texas. The state had been devastated by the Civil War, its economy left in a shambles. Many ranchers and cowboys had ridden off to the war, abandoning their ranches and cattle. By 1866 the state was well into the hangover headache of Reconstruction. Wild, unbranded longhorn cattle were everywhere, and the surviving cowboys who had drifted back were hanging around with nothing to do.

The men and cattle were both perfect for the task at hand. The cattle were descended from the Spanish cattle brought to the New World by Cortez 350 years earlier. Their fierceness and durability let them thrive in the hostile environment of Mexico and the U.S. Southwest. Story is believed to have paid $6 apiece for his thousand of them.

The men were cowboys by trade, having learned the business from Mexican cowboys. The design of their hats and boots and other equipment, along with their vocabulary, all borrowed heavily from the Spanish. It was said that Cortez made a practice of branding his cowboys, presumably to keep them from straying, but this practice never caught on in the states.

The first man Story picked was called Spanish Joe, a Mexican Indian skilled at tracking, reading the prairie and the weather, and communicating with various Indian tribes. Most of the other twenty-four men he picked were battle-hardened veterans of the Confederate cavalry. Where he was going, he was going to need experienced fighting men. Exactly where he was planning to go is not known.

Preparation for the drive, hiring the men, obtaining the cattle, horses, and supplies, took up the month of July. Each cowboy got six horses, three broken and three to be broken on the trip. The cattle were branded with the ox-yoke brand. In early August, the whole outfit finally got moving up the Sedalia Trail toward Kansas. The Sedalia Trail was well trampled; a quarter million cattle moved over it from Texas to Kansas that year.

As they set out, the drovers followed the custom of

Facing page: Dinnertime at the roundup wagon, 1897.

DIANE ENSIGN

pushing the cattle hard the first four or five days to get them out of their home territory and tired enough to keep from running off. After the first few days, the men settled into the routine of letting the cattle graze at the beginning of each day, but keeping them drifting as grazed. At noon they were rested for an hour and allowed to drink, if water was available. In the afternoon they would be driven to a bed ground selected by Story and Spanish Joe.

The chuck wagon moved ahead of the herd to the night's camp. Meals for the cowboys came twice a day, once before dawn and again after dark when the cattle had been bedded and the horses taken care of. The men said they had "two suppers."

At night the men took turns riding around the herd, two men at a time, moving in opposite directions. They sang as they went, and though their music may not have been melodious to the human ear, it was soothing for the cattle. It kept them from getting spooked and stampeding. Many old traditional western songs such as "Streets of Laredo" were said to be centuries-old sea chanteys with new words appropriate for the plains.

Stampedes and river crossings were two of the major hazards. It was said that 1866 was a wet year, and the herd had to cross six major rivers running at full crest. To get the cattle across, the riders bunched them up and hurried them forward so they were in the water before they knew it.

Another potential hazard was Indians. The first part of the drive avoided the Comanche and Apache territory to the west and escaped any Indian trouble. In Oklahoma, the drive was approached by Cherokees, who were peaceful but a little annoyed at the volume of traffic through their territory. They wanted 10¢ a head for passage of the herd, and they wanted to ride through the herd to look for their own cattle that might have strayed. These terms were readily agreed to. The third demand, however, went unmet. They wanted the herd to stay on the main trail. This was not possible because the many cattle that had passed had denuded the land along the main trail.

When the drive reached Kansas, it struck a harder obstacle. This was a gang of Jayhawkers—leftover guerrillas from the Civil War. They were said to be "hard-bitten and murderous." They were heavily armed, and they far outnumbered Story's men. They wanted $4 a head to let the cattle pass. Some of the earlier drives had fought and won or lost, some paid, some abandoned their herds. To the surprise of his cowboys, Story calmly ordered the herd turned back into Oklahoma, and then west.

Just what went on in Story's mind at this point is not known. He may have intended originally to sell the herd in Kansas and then ride on by himself to Montana. His men apparently were under the impression that this was the case. Certainly he knew he could find a ready market in Montana. Cattle trading in and out of the western valleys had been going on there for years, but the new population brought in by the mining strikes would be needing more beef. In camp the first night after turning back, he told the drovers his plan as of that moment. He said he was going to take the herd to Montana, and any man who didn't want to go could draw his pay. They all went.

They drove the herd west until they were beyond Kansas, and then swung north to intersect the Oregon Trail west of Fort Leavenworth. Story left the herd and rode into Fort Leavenworth to make some purchases. He must have still had some greenbacks sewn into his clothes, for in Leavenworth he purchased fifteen big wagons loaded with supplies that would bring a premium price in Montana, along with five teams of oxen to pull each one, and he hired bull whackers to drive them.

Story was also blessed at Leavenworth with one of the many lucky events that occurred on the drive. A shipment of new breech-loading Remington rifles was on hand, and Story bought all thirty of them after a

Meals for the cowboys came twice a day, once before dawn and again after dark when the cattle had been bedded and the horses taken care of.

Facing page: Longhorns on the drive.

demonstration. This was still the age of the muzzle-loader, and a man with a breech-loader was king.

When he got back to the herd with the wagon train, Story called a halt. He had brought fresh food for a banquet, and he issued the men the new rifles. They tried them out and pronounced them first rate. The Indian country to the north may have looked a little less formidable with these rifles at hand.

The drive proceeded to Fort Laramie, the beginning of the Bozeman Trail. At Laramie, the Army tried to talk Story out of his trip. Indian troubles were serious and getting worse, they said. He and his herd would be sitting ducks. But he hadn't come that far to turn back. He pressed on. Story ordered the chuck wagon to stay back where it could be protected, and detailed three sharpshooters to protect the horse herd.

Indians were not the first problem the men ran into.

Right: Pioneer photographer L.A. Huffman called this "The nighthawk in his nest."

Below: Cattle drive across the Powder River, late 19th century.

L.A. HUFFMAN PHOTO, MONTANA HISTORICAL SOCIETY

L.A. HUFFMAN PHOTO, MONTANA HISTORICAL SOCIETY

As they headed up the trail, the season moved on into late September. Small streams were all dried up. After crossing the Cheyenne River, they would find no water for eighty miles. If any cattle were to survive, they would have to make it across this stretch in three days, averaging close to twenty-seven miles a day with no water. Their average distance covered during the entire drive was fifteen miles a day.

Some luck at least: the moon was full, and they could keep moving on into the night. By the middle of the second day, the cattle were lolling their tongues and bawling continuously. Water was low even for the men and horses. That the animals were too dry to graze, and with thirty miles still to go. They went into the third day with the weaker cattle falling behind. Story himself rode behind, moving along as many of the weak ones as he could. The cattle's ribs were sticking out. The men were haggard with bloodshot eyes and cracked lips. They pushed the cattle all night, and at daybreak they came to the valley of the Powder River. The cattle smelled the water and tried to stampede, but they were too feeble and couldn't run very fast. When they hit the water they jumped right in. A rest stop was called so the cows could eat and drink and eat and drink.

With the dry country crossed, it was time to worry about Indians. Some days previous, they had started passing graves of people killed by Indians. The first attack on the drive occurred the first night out of the Powder River camp.

A small band of Indians came into camp whooping and shooting arrows. Two of Story's men were hit by arrows and the Indians drove off a small bunch of cattle. Story and one man chased after them until the Indians turned around and chased them back. Story then regrouped, took most of his men and went back out. They recaptured all the cattle except one the Indians had butchered.

As they continued up the trail, they saw more graves. Smoke signals drifted up from the hills. Still, no further attack came, possibly because the word had got out about the fast-shooting rifles and the men who knew how to use them.

They reached Fort Phil Kearney on October 10. The commanding officer ordered Story to remain there until he had at least fifty men in his party. Story waited, but not patiently. It was late in the year—not likely that additional wagon trains would come along. Nevertheless, Story followed orders, keeping his party at least three miles from the fort, waiting for other travelers to come. He had his men build corrals to protect the horses and cattle from Indians—a good idea, because an attack was not long in coming. The corrals saved the stock but one man was fatally pin-cushioned with arrows.

Other, larger attacks were sure to follow, supplies were getting short, and the Texans weren't equipped to handle cold weather. Story explained things to his men and called for a vote. All but one man voted to defy the army and head north. The one dissenter is one of the few of Story's men whose name is known. George Dow. After Dow's "no" vote, Story ordered him disarmed, tied up, and put on a horse. Despite his druthers, the trussed-up Dow rode with them when they moved the herd out that night after dark. Three days out, they untied Dow and let him vote again—he could either continue on, or go back to the fort. He changed his vote.

In the 75 miles between Fort Phil Kearney and Fort C.F. Smith, Story's party moved only at night, and grazed the herd during the day. They didn't see any Indians, but the farther they went, the more graves they saw.

Pete Story with the saddlebags given to his great-grandfather, Nelson Story, by Plenty Coups, Chief of the Crow.

The destination for the cattle was at the junction of the Yellowstone and Shields rivers, near present-day Livingston.

Pete Story, Nelson's descendant, said it was on this part of the trip that Nelson had his best piece of luck. The great Sioux chief Red Cloud was camped only five miles from the Bozeman Trail with hundreds of warriors, but the Story party was not detected. If it had been, Pete Story says, the tale probably would have to be told by somebody besides him. Pete speculated that the cold weather of late October kept the warriors near their lodge fires. If the drive had not got a late start, if the Army had not held it up at Fort Phil Kearney, Pete might not be here to tell us the story.

But he is. Once past C.F. Smith, the party had only one more small skirmish, one more man pin-cushioned to death within fifty miles of their destination.

The destination for the cattle was at the junction of the Yellowstone and Shields rivers, near present-day Livingston. Once there, Story put one of his men in charge of building cabins and corrals, and pressed on to Bozeman with his frieght wagons and a few of the cattle he wanted to sell. He arrived in Bozeman on December 9. By January 1, he and his wife Ellen, who had been waiting for him in Bozeman, opened a store to sell the goods he brought from Fort Leavenworth.

Pete Story points out that his great-grandfather didn't leave much of a record, no diaries, and no more than a few paragraphs about the events of his cattle drive. As Pete said regarding his great-grandfather, "A lot of what we think we know we don't know." The events of the drive I have given here are the closest we can come to the facts and reflect the family history of the event, scant though it is. With a rare exception, we don't know the names of his cowboys or what happened to them. Tommy Thompson, the man he left in charge of building the ranch, kept working for Story until his death in 1878. He drowned trying to save a couple of drunken cowboys in a river. Nelson, though perhaps not the most sentimental of men, named his second son, Pete's grandfather, after Thompson.

Things changed rapidly in the Yellowstone Valley in the years after Story's drive. The buffalo vanished. The Crow Indian Reservation, which originally included most of the land south of the Yellowstone River, shrank eastward in big jumps. When the country got tamer, the Story ranch established a winter camp near present-day Silesia. In the fall, cattle were trailed down to the lower country.

The winter camps were a refuge for some of the old men around the country who needed a place to hole up. Pete's grandfather remembered going to the camp as a young boy and seeing these old-timers, one of whom was that esteemed early citizen, Liver-Eating Johnson. He knew Indian stories that could make the kids' eyes bug out.

Civilization came on relentlessly, and by 1886, eight passenger trains a day were running both ways up and down the Yellowstone valley. In that famous winter of 1886 when most of the cattle in Montana starved and froze, Nelson Story didn't need anybody to send him a post card (as artist Charles Russell did for *his* boss) telling him about the condition of his herd. He could get on the train in Bozeman and be at his winter camp in a few hours. He took charge personally during that winter, moving cattle around to patches of exposed grass.

This strategy saved two thirds of the herd but Story was said to be "haggard and discouraged" by the experience. Two or three years later he sold his main herd—17,000 head. His entrepreneurial skills did not got to waste, however; he made money in banking and flour mills; and a steamboat he owned paid more than all he made in over twenty years of cattle ranching, he said.

In 1872 he went to California, fell in love with it, and bought three blocks of what was to become downtown Los Angeles. "One of the more prosperous branches of the family still lives there," Pete said.

As for the Story ranch, it continues. It is not likely

that any other ranch has undergone more changes while remaining in the same family. "Each generation has changed it," Pete said. "It's a helluva lot smaller than it once was." In good times, the ranch has tended to expand. On the other hand, "When we get our ears pinned back, it shrinks." A major part of the ranch was for a long time located just east of Bozeman on land that Nelson had purchased with Civil War scrip. This scrip was given to Union veterans of the Civil War so they could buy land. A lot of them sold the scrip instead. The Story holdings also included twenty-four acres that Nelson donated for the campus of Montana State University.

From the original longhorns, the ranch went to Herefords around 1900, and then later to sheep. Many ranchers went to sheep for a while, but then the price of wool dropped from 75¢ to 5¢ a pound. "That just about broke the whole outfit," Pete said.

In 1935, wool was 8¢, and Storys held onto theirs rather than sell for that price. In 1936, Pete said, "My dad put on a Brooks Brothers suit, waxed his mustache, and went to Boston to see his bankers. They showed him a rayon factory. He was the first sheepman to stare at the future." In 1939 the ranch switched back to cattle, Black Angus this time.

Pete bought the ranch from his father, Malcolm. One of the marks Pete made on the ranch was to sell the land near Bozeman and buy land adjoining the part of the ranch near Yankee Jim Canyon. This consolidated the holdings into a compact piece. It also eliminated having to haul cattle back and forth between the Bozeman land and the Paradise Valley land. Pete recently sold the ranch to his son, Nelson.

This latest Nelson Story is much more of a cowboy than his father, said the father. Pete said he was never much of a cowboy, never had more than three horses on the place, and probably didn't need two of them. "If I could do it on foot, I did," he said. "I know how to rope but I don't like to rope in front of cowboys because it makes them giggle." He said he liked to gather cattle with a couple of dogs and his kids. Pete would drive the pickup, and the kids and dogs would drive the cattle. If they missed any, they'd have to hike back and find them. "It encouraged efficiency," Pete said.

He said that when he took the ranch over, it needed a mechanic and a welder and somebody to keep an eye on the books more than it needed a cowboy. Pete even committed the social error of not attending his neighbors' branding. "I didn't have ten days to take off," he said. He didn't need a big crew to do his own branding. He just hired four teenagers from town. "They didn't need to know what they were doing," he said. The small amateur crew was enough because Pete used a branding table, a mechanical device that eliminates roping and other cowboy performances.

Despite a cautious and conservative upbringing, the new Nelson Story has thrown back to the cowboy line. No more branding table. Now cowboys rope the Story calves and drag them to the fire like they did in the days of Nelson I. One difference is the music. No old sea chanteys at the Story brandings.

Pete described the branding music. "It sounds like an operation without any anesthetic. Screaming into the microphone. They drink beer and listen to horrible music and have a great time. Cowgirls come and get right down into the manure.

"One year there were fifty people here for branding. Maybe ten of them did anything. The feed bill alone was enough to hire four good men to do the work."

Progress has made other marks too. When he was a boy, Pete said, it took twenty men to run the ranch, and fifty horses, including twenty or thirty draft horses for haying. "Now Nelson does it all himself. With his blue heeler."

Ray Krone

DANIEL N. VICHOREK

Consumer warning regarding Ray Krone: The author is aware that children old enough to go to school in 1994 are fluent in the use of foul language. However, I know it troubles them to hear adults talk like the kids do. Political correctness probably demands that such little tikes not be exposed to some of the non-standard language Krone has picked up in his many years on the range. He uses expressions such as "like shit through a horn," and "as full of shit as a young owl," and even "tight-assed and popcorn." So don't read this, kids.

Anybody who craves to know about cowboys in Montana should talk to Ray Krone. Krone—whose family owns two ranching operations, one at the foot of the Bighorns south of Hardin and the other near Augusta—is a cowboy of the old school. Or as he puts it, with characteristic clarity, "I'm a dinosaur."

Regarding cowboys, he said, "There aren't more than twenty-five outside cowboys in Montana, and I know damned near all of them." Not only that, but he's related to some of the best ones; his sons Lance and Larry, for example, and their kids. Krone draws a line between outside cowboys, who know the old traditional ways of working with cattle and horses out in the open, and modern types who would rather be in a pickup or some other warm dry place. "They don't know if a cow roosts in a tree or sleeps on the ground," he said.

Krone may be the first dinosaur in his family. His father, known and remembered to Montana cow people as P.R. Krone, was born in Missouri and came west to work on the railroad in about 1905. Upon reaching Billings, P.R. and another young fellow traveling with him discovered that their financial circumstances had been reduced to a dime apiece. They repaired to a nearby saloon where their dimes would buy them a beer and access to the free lunch that came with a beer in those days.

They muddled through somehow, and P.R. went to work in the sugar factory. The other fellow went to work for the railroad and eventually became a conductor. Family history does not record how P.R. Krone came into contact with Frank Heinrich, owner of the Antler Ranch on the Crow Reservation south of Hardin, but he did. He went to work as a an apprentice cowboy.

For a farm boy from Missouri, the Antler Ranch may have looked a little overwhelming. A million and a half acres and cows to fill it up, horses by the hundreds and, as Ray said, "old greasy cowboys," some of whom had ridden up the Chisholm Trail with cattle from Texas. Time seemed to be standing still on the Antler: nothing much had changed since 1890. Or 1870. Krone said the Crow Reservation was the last stronghold of the big cow outfits. Ranchers were able to lease very large tracts of land on the reservation and operate cow outfits on the open range in the old way. The Antler alone held lease to about half the entire Crow Reservation.

Growing up on a farm in Missouri did not offer much training for working on the Antler. Personal characteristics were important. One essential thing P.R. had going for him, according to Ray, was "grim determination." When the elder Krone went to work for the Antler, all the land in the vicinity was open range—no fences. Each ranch had its roundup wagon where the cowboys ate and slept as they moved the herd from place to place.

"Thousands of cattle ran loose with no fences, and everybody got their strays back. These days, the country is all fenced up, and if a cow gets on the wrong side of the fence the sheriff will be up there looking into it.

"It was a wonderful life for them," Krone said, referring to all the people involved on the big ranches. The work was hard, the days long, the pay low, the weather subject to severe variation, but that added up to a great life. Krone said the old cowboy way of life

Facing page: The Krone ranch on Flat Creek near Augusta.

"Our cattle are so wild we can't even catch 'em."

lingered on the big ranches on the Crow long after it had vanished elsewhere. This way of life was based on honesty and respect and fair dealing, he said. "If you needed some hay, you went over to your neighbor's haystack and took some. If you saw him later, you'd tell him about it, and replace it when you could. What would happen if you tried that today?"

And there was loyalty. "Back in those days the outfit a guy worked for was part of his self-image. No cowboy would badmouth his boss or the ranch. And the ranches took care of their men. You don't see that kind of loyalty today."

Men and cattle were not the only things on the open range. Thousands of wild horses ran loose in the Pryor Mountains, and Frank Heinrich, owner of the Antler, decided to catch them. There was only one fence in the vicinity at that time, Ray said, and that one ran along the old highway between Hardin and Billings. Heinrich had his men take down two miles of the fence, intending to chase the horses through the gap and then to close it up behind them to keep them in the lower country where they could be caught at leisure. P.R. Krone was there, and told Ray what happened.

There were a hundred men. Fifty were supposed to chase the horses down, and the other fifty would make sure they went through the fence and then close it up behind them. The fifty drivers were in place before daylight. When it got light, they mounted up and started driving the horses.

The distance from the Pryors to the old highway is quite a few miles, so it was mid-morning before P.R. Krone and all the men who were waiting saw a tall cloud of dust coming up fast. Soon the horses were in view, surging down like the tide, maybe 5,000 horses coming on fast.

"There was every damn kind of horse you can imagine, every size and shape and color, ponies, work horses, mules." Something about the plan was not just right, and the horses took alarm and turned back. Nobody could do a thing about it. The riders roped ten or twelve of them that had saddle marks, and most of these probably had gone wild from the Antler to begin with, Ray said. The rest of them got away, and P.R. said he was glad. "What a sight to see," Ray said.

Most of the cowboy jobs were seasonal. The men would be hired in April or May when the roundup wagons were pulled out on the range, and let go in the fall, sometimes near Christmas, when the work was all done. They tended to blow their pay and spend the winter in a livery barn, getting their meals where they could. When they were broke, some of them would drift back to the ranch and spend the winter in the bunkhouse, eating for free and maybe doing a few chores. Riding the grubline, this was sometimes called.

P.R. Krone proved an apt student of cowboy science and worked his way up from Missouri farmboy to general manager of the Antler. After he had been manager for a while, he had the opportunity to buy a smaller ranch nearby. Courtesy required him to ask the owner of the Antler if he wanted to buy the place, but the answer was no, so the Krone family got into the cattle business for itself.

When Krone bought his own ranch, the owner of the Antler asked him to stay on as general manager, and he did. He then had to hire someone to operate the Krone place while he ran the Antler.

Later on, P.R. had to help disperse the estate when the Antler owner died. There were 16,000 cattle on the Antler, and the only logical buyer was E.L. Dana, who owned another large ranch nearby. A problem developed, however, when lawyers and other high-pressure types showed up. Dana was not exactly a timid man after spending his life on the range, growing up with the country, but he was accustomed to doing things in a

Western fashion where a handshake stood for a contract. He was afraid of the lawyers. P.R. went to Dana's ranch and found the old man watering with a garden hose out behind the house. He reassured Dana, invested a little of his own credibility, and persuaded him to buy the whole bunch.

Ray Krone was born in Hardin in 1924, and grew up on the family ranch. He developed a certain originality in speech and manner. When he proposed marriage, for example, he promised his intended, "We'll have diamonds as big as horse turds. Or vice-versa." Ray and his new wife Ruth spent their first year of marriage in a house under the rimrock just outside Fort Smith. Snakes liked it there. When he had to walk across the grass near his house after dark, Ray would throw his rope out in front of him to locate the rattlers. He bagged twelve in the year they lived there. He thought it was a good sign that his wife didn't leave him, just because of the snakes alone. "A lot of women wouldn't put up with that," he said.

In 1945, the Krones expanded their operation by purchasing a ranch southwest of Augusta. "This Augusta area was originally sheep country," Krone said. "It was common knowledge that you couldn't winter cattle because the weather was too rough. Everybody cusses this country because of the wind. Me, if the wind quits blowing in the winter, I'm down on my prayer bones asking for it to start again." The Krones rely on the wind to keep the grass exposed for the cattle. They don't feed any hay unless they have to. All calving is done on the ranch near Hardin. Steers are moved to the Augusta place as yearlings and sold when they are three years old and weigh about 1,200 pounds

"We're the last ones that sell these big steers," Ray said. "Sometimes we have a hard time sellin' 'em." The cattle business, he explained, is geared to calves that weigh 600 or 700 pounds, and which are then taken to a feedlot and fed until they weigh 1,100 pounds or so, after which they are slaughtered. The American housewife has a major role in determining how big cattle should be when they are slaughtered. She has a husband and 2.3 children, and she needs beef cuts of a certain size. The desired size does not come from a three-year-old steer the size of an average saddle horse.

Krone said the housewife doesn't know what she is missing. "Beef doesn't even get its flavor until it's two years old," he said. "What people think of as beef is really just big veal. Actually," he said, "we should get a premium for our beef. It's a hundred percent pure. No hormone implants, no drugs in the meat." The Krones brand, castrate and vaccinate their cattle when they are calves and don't mess with them after that. No pregnancy testing, certainly no artificial insemination, none of the stuff that takes up a lot of time on most ranches. "These days a lot of ranchers use numbered ear tags so they can keep cow number one with calf number one and so on. This modern way of doing things is not my bag," Ray said.

Somewhere out there, Ray theorizes, there must be a specialty beef outlet of some sort that would appreciate first quality, non-chemicalized, man-sized T-bones that have the tang of the open range on them, rather than a faint hint of mother's milk and corn meal. Representatives of such outfits can get hold of him any time, Ray said. (Author's note: I ate one and have been feeling like breaking down the fences ever since.)

The Krones also don't spend a lot of effort helping their cows have calves. "Our cows calve outside on the grass," Ray said. "A cow should know how to have a calf."

Krones don't even dehorn their cattle, and the placid expression most cows have is missing on the horned critters that grow on the Krone ranch. "Our cattle are so wild we can't even catch 'em," Ray said. That's the way the Krones like them. "Old gentle cattle

GARRY WUNDERWALD

"One second you were lookin' at their butts and the next you were lookin' at their faces."

In the chutes.

are hard to handle," Ray said. Wild cattle, on the other hand, can be moved around by someone on horseback at a good pace.

Back in the days when there actually was train service to Augusta, the Krones trailed their cattle seven miles from their ranch to the loading point. Getting the wild steers to go the way they wanted them to go was sometimes a chore. The best way to handle steers, Krone said, is to let them follow a cow. "It's the sex thing," Ray said. Even though steers are castrated as calves, they retain enough interest in an adult female to follow her anywhere.

For some years, the Krones had a faithful old cow that they used to lead the steers to market. She was known affectionately as "Mrs. Moo," and Ray described her as a "crossbred old red cow." When it was time to move the steers, Ray would put a halter on Mrs. Moo, get on his horse, and take off with Mrs. Moo running alongside at a gallop, the steers surging along behind. The drive went down road lanes fenced on both sides, and as Ray said, when things worked out right, "They went through there like shit through a horn." Even when the drive was going well, everybody was a little tense, a condition Ray referred to as "tight-ass and popcorn."

Sometimes, things didn't go so smoothly. Once in a while, for example, all the steers would suddenly turn and face back the way they came. "One second you were lookin' at their butts and the next you were lookin' at their faces." Ray said. "You'd think there would be one of them that wouldn't get the word, but no, every single one of them would turn at the same time."

The steers couldn't run back because their way was blocked by riders in the narrow passage, but they could break down the fences and run off. The Krones could hear it when the fence wire started to stretch: the fences would go "ark ark ark," indicating they weren't going to

Movie Cowboys

In the early days of motion pictures, Hollywood often hired real cowboys to work in the movies. Two men achieved the dual honor of winning both rodeo championships and Academy Awards.

The first of these was Yakima Canutt, who started his rodeo career in 1910 and continued into the '20s, winning championships in several events and becoming champion All-Around Cowboy. He went into the movie business in the early '20s and became famous as a stunt man in rough and tumble western movies, eventually winning an Oscar.

The second man to win both in Hollywood and the rodeo was Ben Johnson. Johnson was from Oklahoma, and in 1940 somebody hired him to haul a load of horses to movie set in California. Somebody important spotted him and hired him to do stunt work. Eventually he began acting and in his career performed in more than 80 films including classics such as *Shane*. He got his Oscar in 1971 for his role in *The Last Picture Show*. Eighteen years earlier, in 1953, he won a world championship in team roping. Today he makes his home at least part of the time near Ennis, where he is in the real estate business.

—*Moments in Rodeo*, written and published by Ernest Tooke, Box 495, Ekalaka, Montana 59324

take much more strain. The possibility of the fence breaking and the steers escaping was always in mind as the cowboys used Mrs. Moo and got the lead portion of the herd going the right way, followed by the rest. "I

Cowboys catching their mounts in the roundup cavvy, in rope corral.

liked the drive," Ray said. "It was cowboy work." Ray said 1,200 head of 1,200-pound steers filled up the lane between the fences for a mile.

Ray is still annoyed at some spectators who made light of the Krone's cattle drive. "They said, 'Look at that, those Krones need that old cow to get their steers to market.' I'd like to turn those steers loose out on the flat and let those guys try to catch 'em."

One year Mrs. Moo showed up for work with a crack in her hoof, and Ray had a nightmare vision of what could happen: Mrs. Moo going lame during the drive, the steers, suddenly without a leader, going through the fences and heading for the hills. To fend off this possibility, Ray telephoned around to see if there was anybody who still knew how to install ox shoes. In the early days of Montana, oxen pulled the bulk of the freight wagons and were often fitted with two-piece shoes, one half for each side of the foot. That was a while back, though, and Ray couldn't find anybody who knew how to put shoes on a cow, much less find any shoes to do it with. Finally some pragmatist suggested putting a horse shoe on her, which worked just fine, though they had to throw her down to do it. "She wore that shoe a long time," Ray said. "I often wondered what some drunk cowboy would have thought if he saw the tracks of an animal with three cow feet and one horse foot." Finally, the grim reaper came even for Mrs. Moo, and Ray found her dead one day.

"I like to have cried," he said. Other cows took Mrs. Moo's place over the years, but none is remembered quite as sentimentally as she.

These days, the Krones have no need for Mrs. Moo. When it's time to ship, trucks come to the Krone ranch and load the cattle. "I hate those possum-bellied trucks," Ray said. He thinks trucks are harder on the cattle than the trains used to be. "I raise these cattle and I like 'em and I don't want 'em abused," he said. For their part, the Krone cattle have had some revenge on those possum-bellied trucks: in the past some of the ones with horns have wound up on the top deck where they poked holes in the aluminum roof "until it looked like a sieve."

One precaution with the Krone cattle is to get them into small pens if you're going to pen them up, Ray said. That way, they don't have enough power to take the fences down. A feedlot in Iowa learned this lesson the hard way. The lot had a freshly arrived bunch of the Krones' semi-wild beef in a pen, and one of the attendants came along with "a little rattlin' thingamajig" that they used for feeding the animals. There were more than enough steers to take the fence down, which they did, and ran wild out in the cornfields for a while. The corn was tall, Ray said, and the Iowa cowboys had a dickens of a time trying to catch those mountain-grown bovines. "They finally had to shoot the last two," he said.

There is no certainty about how long the Krones will be able to continue to sell three-year-old wild cattle. "I hope we don't have to change while I'm alive," Ray said. He pointed out numerous advantages to his system of selling older cattle, besides the quality of the beef. He cited the original wisdom of P.R. Krone: "My old dad had the ability to look through things," he said. For example, if cattle prices get so low that you can't afford to sell, you don't have to, if you don't have to sell them while they're calves. You can save them until the next year. The wisdom of this flexibility was proved during the Depression when cattle prices dropped so low that shipping charges were greater than the value of the cattle. When that happened, Krone said, his father "gritted his teeth" and held the cattle for another year.

Besides being efficient cow factories, the Krone ranches are highly photogenic. When Madison Avenue wants to evoke western nostalgia and get people to smoke a particular brand of cigarettes, for example, photo-graphers come out to the Krone ranches, which are not all cluttered up with a lot of modern stuff to ruin the antique ambiance. Millions of people all over the world have seen portions of the Krone ranches in photographs of the Marlboro Man, although computer manipulation of the photographs changed the landscape around in ways not necessarily foreseen by God or approved by Krone.

In the process of providing backdrops, however, Ray and his family got well acquainted with one of the models known to the world as the Marlboro Man. "He's no fake," Ray said. "He sure looks good on a horse." The last time they saw him, though, his age was creeping up and he had to wear a girdle to simulate a youthful midsection. Later he had to get a hearing aid and some false teeth. He didn't have to worry about his hair because he always wears a hat.

Ray and his wife Ruth said they raised their sons to be cowboys. The younger Krones, Larry and Lance, both make their livings on the Krone ranches. Further, Ray said, a new generation of cowpersons is well on the way. "We've got ten grandkids— six bulls and four heifers," he said. When these grandchildren are about seven years old, Ray starts taking them out on a horse, showing them how to do things. "One of these days they'll wake up and be good cowboys," Ray said. He can't imagine any higher calling.

DANIEL N. VICHOREK

Ray Krone, dinosaur of the cattle business.

Leo Plain Feather

Ray Krone, whom I am glad to accept as an objective authority, told me the world has come to such a sad state that there are no more than twenty-five real cowboys left in Montana. He said one of the best is Leo Plain Feather of Fort C.F. Smith. I visited Mr. Plain Feather at his house and told him what Krone said. "We'll have to give Ray some sort of reward," he said.

We sat down to talk over the cowboy business. He told me that he was born about three miles down the Bighorn River from Fort Smith near a place called the Spotted Rabbit Crossing. When he was a boy, one of the major ranches in the vicinity, the Dana Ranch, crossed its cattle at the Spotted Rabbit Crossing. While the roundup wagon was in the vicinity, Plain Feather and other kids would go over for supper.

Young Leo fell in love with the cowboy life. His grandfather gave him a rope, and he roped the family poultry until he wore all the feathers off their necks. At thirteen he went to work as a horse wrangler for Wilcutt's ranch, the Grapevine, named after the wild grapes that grow along the creeks where that ranch was located, west of the Bighorn River. The Grapevine at its peak covered about 100,000 acres and ran up to 10,000 cattle, Plain Feather said.

"I worked thirty-five years for H.W. Wilcutt Jr. He practically raised me." In his years with Wilcutt, Plain Feather said, he did every job from the lowest to the highest. The lowest was horse wrangler. The horse wrangler's job was to take care of the horses, which could number up to 150, and to be a handyman, chop wood, carry water, help the cook. The highest job was "running the wagon," meaning that he was foreman in charge of all the operations carried out from the wagon. The Grapevine Ranch was one of the last to operate a traditional ranching operation with a mess wagon.

Plain Feather recalled the annual cycle with the wagon on the Grapevine. Normally, he said, they'd pull the wagon out in April. Actually, the term "roundup wagon" referred to two wagons that traveled together: the mess wagon, pulled by four horses and hauling a stove and equipment for the cook, and the bed wagon, hauling the men's bedrolls, always just called "beds," and all the other possessions they had with them. These possessions were scant, often whimsically referred to as their "forty years' gatherin's." Usually about ten or twelve men stayed with the wagon all summer, unless they quit or maybe went to Hardin to celebrate the Fourth of July. The crew would include a horse wrangler, a "nighthawk" to take care of the horses at night and to chauffeur the bed wagon, a cook, and the boss.

One of the boss's responsibilities was to assign horses to the men. Normally the men were required to ride horses owned by the ranch, and if they had personal horses these were left behind when the wagon pulled out. Normally, Plain Feather said, the boss would know some of the horses and some of the men, but others were strangers to him. Nevertheless, it was his job to match men and horses so that difficult horses went to good riders who could handle them, tamer horses went to less accomplished hands, and so on. When dealing with strangers, the boss had to be a good judge of men and horses. "Just one of the things you learn," Plain Feather said.

The boss would go into the horse herd, called a cavvy, and rope eight to ten horses for each man. The men would use these same horses all season, and were responsible for being able to recognize them and catch them in the dark of early morning when the work began.

When the horses were all assigned and other organizational tasks taken care of, the wagons would go to the lower portion of the ranch, the winter range, to gather cattle and move them up to higher country. The cattle were gathered in the old traditional way, with a "circle."

Fall roundup of Herefords on the Grapevine Ranch.

DANIEL N. VICHOREK

Leo Plain Feather with his stud,
Richelieu.

The wagon boss, along with the other riders—rode around the cattle to be gathered, dropping a man off here and there until the scattered cattle were surrounded. Then, following the boss's instructions as to speed and direction, the men rode toward the cattle, hazing them in a circular bunch to a specified spot. The properly executed circle, according to some, is a beauty to witness, all the men and horses working together like clockwork over uneven terrain to bring the cattle to the right place.

Gathering the cattle and moving them off the winter range usually took a couple weeks, Plain Feather said. Once the cattle were moved, there wasn't much to do until branding time. It was a rainy time of the year, but if the weather was good sometimes they'd fill up some slack time by poisoning prairie dogs. Being cowboys, they did this from horseback: bags of poisoned oats draped over the horse, the horse moving from hole to hole, stopping, the rider dribbling a few oats into the hole, and moving on. Not very demanding work. Not like branding.

Branding has always been a festive occasion on most of the ranches. Technology tried to change the old way of doing things, bringing in the squeeze chute and the branding table, but even in 1993 these inventions were widely scorned. The damned things would do away with roping! The outrage is hardly believable. As Ray Krone said, "Why would you be a cowboy if you couldn't rope?" Or as Plain Feather said, "I like to eat but I'd rather rope."

They didn't encourage technology on the Grapevine Ranch. Along about the middle of May, the cowboys gathered the cattle and began branding. The ten or twelve men working for the outfit would be joined by "reps," men from other nearby ranches who joined in the work and looked after any cattle belonging to the ranches they represented.

Sometimes, Plain Feather said, the branding crew might number as many as twenty-five men. In the traditional fashion, the Grapevine branded out in the open.

Calves were roped from horseback and dragged to the branding fire, where two-man crews of "wrasslers" held them down while they were branded. The Grapevine normally had four crews of wrasslers working at a time. Roping being the great fun that it is, everybody wanted a turn, and Leo let each man rope for an hour at a time. The experienced ropers slipped easily in and out of the herd without creating a big disturbance, unlike greenhorns who tend to charge in and scare everything. Another one of the things you learn, Leo said. He said they branded up to 225 calves a day at the Grapevine, with the work lasting three or four weeks.

When branding was over, the cattle were turned loose on the summer range. Bulls were parceled out, one for each twenty cows, and the men assigned to line shacks scattered them around properly. The line shacks were cabins where cowboys stayed while cattle were on the range nearby. The cowboys kept an eye on the cattle and made sure they were where they were supposed to be. A wagon with a four-horse team would drop salt off at established salt grounds a couple of times during the summer.

With all these operations in place, the mess wagon could stay in one place for some time while the cowboys put up wild hay for the horses, fixed fences and took care of other miscellaneous chores.

By the latter part of July, it was time to gather the "beef." The "beef" consisted of the three- and four-year-old cattle that were to be sold for slaughter that year. The Grapevine Herefords usually weighed 1,500 or 1,600 pounds when they were this age, two or three times the size of the beef calves of the 1990s.

It normally took a month to gather the beef, which then had to be trailed sixty miles to a rail siding for shipping. Shipping usually took place about mid-September. After that, it was time to move the cattle back to winter pasture. Calves would be weaned from their mothers and the smaller ones taken to the lower country where the winter would be easier. The older ones were kept where pickups could be used to bring them supplemental feed.

Along about Thanksgiving, the season was over and the wagons returned to ranch headquarters. The normal practice was to lay off the cowboys when the work was all done. Some of them would be back the next year.

Leo worked for the Grapevine until it was sold in 1967. When the place sold, the mess wagon went to the Buffalo Bill Museum in Cody, Wyoming, where it is on display.

Running the wagon for the Grapevine was a great experience, Plain Feather said. "When I was a kid, I set two goals," he said. "The first was to run a wagon. I fulfilled that one at Wilcutts'. My second goal was to run a big ranch. I fulfilled that one after Wilcutt sold out, down at the Arapaho Ranch."

The Arapaho Ranch is a big ranch owned by the Arapaho Tribe in Wyoming. It runs up to 16,000 cattle. Plain Feather went to work there as cow foreman and got promoted to general manager in two weeks. He stayed on for four years, then returned to the Crow Reservation, where the tribe hired him to run the tribal buffalo herd.

Running a buffalo herd was not on Plain Feather's original to-do list, and some said it couldn't be done anyway. "Guys were telling me, 'You can't corral buffalo'," he said. "One of them said he'd eat his hat if I could do it."

Corralling buffalo turned out not to be so difficult, and only required that plywood be nailed up on the corral so the buffalo could not see out. Plain Feather handled the buffalo much like regular cattle, blood-testing them for disease, vaccinating them, and weaning the calves in the fall. Weaning the calves was part of an effort to get the buffalo to calve every year, which they do not do in the wild. It worked, and in the five years he ran the herd it increased from 75 to 600. Despite this effort, Plain Feather

The wagon boss, along with the other riders—rode around the cattle to be gathered, dropping a man off here and there until the scattered cattle were surrounded.

eventually was afflicted with one of the great banes of public employment—Change of Administration—and out he went.

In the years since then, he has alternated among taking it easy, doing a little spot work here and there, and raising a few horses. The little community of Fort Smith has been a good deal amused over a story about one of Leo's horses. It was a nice pinto, and he normally was in plain view of the road where anybody could see him. One day Jane Fonda drove by and saw him and came in to make Leo an offer. Stories vary about what happened after that. Leo simplified the story for me. "We couldn't make a deal," he said. I asked him where the horse was. "I've got him hid so nobody else will see him," he said.

Like most cowboys, Leo is a married man. He and his wife have seven grown children, not one of which is a cow person. "Thirty-five years and I only got home seven times," he joked. These days, he said, it is easier being a married man on the ranches, because often there are buildings where couples can live.

Leo spends some time thinking about the past, and more time thinking about the future. As for the past, he said, he can close his eyes and see that whole big country where the Wilcutt ranch was. Not long ago he got a friend to fly him over the place. "It's all plowed up now," he said. "It made me sad, kind of sick, to see the old battleground in that shape."

As for the future, he'd like to get back to being a ranch boss. "I get calls and letters all the time from cowboys asking me, 'Why don't you run a ranch?' They'd come from all over if we could run a ranch like we used to do. Good cowboys who know what they're doing.

"I'm from the old school," Plain Feather said. He traced his enrollment in the old school back to the days when he was a kid eating supper at the Dana wagon. He said some of his tutoring was from old-style cowboys who came up from Texas with the herds, their posture permanently altered by riding all that way on "two joints of backbone," as Charlie Russell said.

"I don't like working with the current generation," he said. "They do everything back-asswards. They like to leave town in their pickups about two hours after they should be starting work out here. My grandfather told me, 'If you work for a man, do the best job for him that you can.' And I always have. I've learned a lot and I'd like to pass it on. I'd like to get some young cowboys, and pass on the knowledge from the old school."

If he could get a contract to operate some big ranch with lots of cattle, he could go down to Cody and get that old Grapevine wagon (which he said is still in good shape) and the old school could go back into session.

Until then, keep an eye out for his race horses. There's Dash for Cash, for example, and Wake Up Running. You could bet on them.

Facing page: Branding time on the Grapevine.

Cal's Custom Boots

No cowboy ever wants to be set afoot, but he wants the best boots he can afford on his feet. The world is afloat with a proliferation of factory-made cowboy boots, but like the old-time cowboys, many modern folks want a boot that is handmade and custom built to fit their feet and tastes.

These are the people who come to Dave and Lynn Calcaterra at Cal's Custom Boot Shop in Bozeman. Anybody can buy a pair of Cal's custom boots, but Dave said he caters to cowboys. "We try to keep our prices down to where a cowboy can afford it," he said. "You have to figure that if a cowboy is laying out three hundred dollars for a pair of boots, that's probably a hundred dollars more than he's got."

The other two things a cowboy needs in his boots are style and durability. "They've got to hold up under serious punishment," Dave said. Regarding style, Dave said that cowboys do not necessarily adhere to earth tones in their gear. Sometimes they like black feet on their boots with bright colored tops. He recalled one pair that went out with black feet and canary yellow tops. A cowboy may get bucked off in the rodeo, Dave said, "But he likes to look good doing it."

Boot styles change. Just now, Dave pointed out, chaps are shorter and boots are taller, reaching to near the knee. When chaps get longer, boots get shorter.

Dave and his wife Lynn divide the labor in their shop, turning out between them one pair of boots every day, about 250 pairs a year. The

DANIEL N. VICHOREK

Dave Calcaterra and his fancy footwork.

Calcaterras make cowboy boots in three basic models, Wellington ropers, western riding boots, and lace-up packers. Nearly all their boots are made of cowhide rather than the expensive exotic leather favored by some. "Not many people want to pay $800 for a pair of boots," Dave said.

Beyond the three basic styles, the variations can be nearly infinite. Some models are plain and utilitarian, others fancy. Different versions are designed for everything from bulldogging to the western two-step. "A lady's dancing boot is going to be different than a bulldogger's boot," Dave said.

The basic price for the packers is $200, with the price increasing for various added features, such as taller than normal tops, decorative stitching, and so on. The western riding boots start at $298.

Dave said the bootmaking he and Lynn practice is a combination of traditional methods and hi-tech, with emphasis on the traditional. The boots are hand-formed to a last and sewn and nailed together in the time-honored fashion, but the fancy stitching on the toes is applied by a computer-operated sewing machine.

Making a pair of boots takes 150 separate steps, Dave said. He painstakingly learned each one of those steps by teaching himself bootmaking while he was working in his shoe repair shop in Lewistown. He decided he liked making boots better than repairing them, and opened his bootmaking shop in Bozeman in 1991. "All we do is make boots," he said, though they do repair the ones they make.

Handmade boots are especially desirable for people who have foot problems, such as bunions, or maybe feet of different size, Dave said. People whose feet fall into the standard range may be able to buy a pair of the Calcaterra's boots off the shelf at their shop in Bozeman. Otherwise, they'll have to order a pair, and the wait is usually about ten weeks, Dave said.

Undated, this Huffman photograph shows a roundup herd and horse cavvy at the head of Little Pumpkin Creek. Note the nighthawk's tent in foreground.

KENT & CHARLENE KRONE

A Cowboy Wedding

R.D. Horne was a single man when he came up from Texas to work on the Binion ranch. He hadn't been there long though before he and the rest of the cowboys took a day off and went to Miles City for what he described as a "shoot 'em up weekend." He was playing a little poker in a saloon when he noticed this swell-looking blonde.

One thing led to another, and before the summer was over, they had a date to go to a rodeo in Winnett. That's when he proposed. She said yes, and they decided to get married in the barn at the Binion ranch. Right in front of the bronc pen. "I stood there by the bronc pen with my man, and she was in the back with her women, and came walking to where I was."

They swore their oaths in the prescribed manner, and then were carried off in the back of a ranch wagon chauffeured by Cyndi's parents. "That was my idea," R.D. said. "It was supposed to be like we were riding off into the sunset. It just went out and made a big circle and came back."

For the honeymoon they went into Miles City and had some pizza. "It was a busy time on the ranch," R.D. said, "and I really couldn't get away for a big honeymoon. But I love her like crazy."

I called R.D. in January and asked him how he was holding up to the weather. It was 25 below zero, winds up to 60 miles an hour, and 18 inches of snow. "Not too bad," he said. "Maybe it's about average around here." He also told me that there was going to be another little buckaroo or buckarette on the Binion ranch a little later in the year.

Left: R.D. Horne.

DANIEL N. VICHOREK

The Binion Ranch

When ranch people talk about big ranches in Montana, sooner or later the talk turns to the Binion ranch. Plopped down on 198,000 acres just east of Jordan, the Binion ranch is a sizable chunk of real estate. Originally assembled by purchase of a large number of failed homesteads, the ranch has been primarily a horse ranch. Benny Binion, the man who put the ranch together, was a horse fancier. Greg Sevier, manager of the ranch, said the ranch had 4,000 horses in the early 1970s. "Benny Binion was the only man who ever owned four thousand head of registered quarter horses," he said.

Binion died several years before my visit to the Binion ranch in 1993, but the ranch is still owned by his family, and horses are still a major part of the operation. Sevier said the ranch has 265 brood mares; about 540 horses altogether including the 75 head of saddle-broke riding stock. A major part of the ranch activity is breaking two-year-old colts to ride.

Sevier said he and the two other cowboys on the place start riding the unbroken two-year-old colts in about April, and gradually begin using them for ranch work. Each man is responsible for ten to fifteen colts. Given the size and rough terrain of the Binion ranch and the far scatter of the pastures, a lot of riding is necessary. From about April until November, "at least one man rides every day," Sevier said. The ranch has seven main pastures averaging about ten to fourteen square miles apiece. The biggest pasture is the Breaks, 98 square miles.

Branding begins in mid-May and lasts about a month. The ranch hires some extra help during branding, usually seven to nine people, Sevier said.

The cattle are Angus-longhorn crosses. The longhorn blood makes the cattle good for rodeo stock. They are sold

Left: *Greg Sevier on the Binion Ranch, with his dog Woodrow at the edge of 96,000-acre Missouri Breaks pasture.*

to rodeo producers for use as roping steers, and the Angus blood makes them good for beef when their rodeo careers are over.

Starting about the Fourth of July, seventy to eighty bulls are put out with the cows. Later on, the cows are separated from the bulls and put on to winter pasture, most of which is in the ninety-eight square miles of the ranch that is located in the Missouri Breaks. The Breaks are the rough badland country that runs along the Missouri River. The acreage is measured as seen from above, and the actual surface area is much greater because of the rough terrain. "If they'd iron that country out flat it would go clear to North Dakota," one of the cowboys said.

At the time of my visit, the sole occupants of the Binion ranch were three cowboys: Sevier, R.D. Horne, Clayton Phipps, a maintenance man, and Cyndi Horne, R.D.'s wife. Cyndi was employed to cook for the men, and they agreed she was learning the job pretty well. "She ain't poisoned us yet," said R.D.

R.D. Horne, one of 11 children, was brought up in a ranch family in Texas. He heard the legend of the Binion ranch while he was still in Texas, and then he saw the movie *Lonesome Dove* and decided to come and have a look for himself. At the time of my visit, the other cowboys had him pretty worried about Montana's winter weather. "Forty-two below for two weeks last year," Greg Sevier told him. "And I thought the Texas panhandle had bad weather," Horne said.

DANIEL N. VICHOREK

The crowned heads of the Binion Ranch

Horne said the ranch business is a little different in Montana than in Texas. For example, in Montana, when he wore his spurs into town (Jordan), people made fun of him. Now he takes them off before he goes to town. Other than that, he wears them about all the time. Both Horne and Sevier were wearing their spurs when they took me out for a pickup-truck tour of the Binion ranch. We drove up to the lip of the breaks and looked down in. The coulees were golden with grass under a clear November sky. Far below we could see cattle, and some miles off a sliver of sapphire blue water showed the location of Fort Peck Reservoir.

Cattle spend their winters in the shelter of the breaks, and the cowboys use pickups to deliver supplemental feed pellets daily, and to make sure the water holes are not frozen up. In the winter it is normal to put 200 miles a day on the pickup used for feeding, Sevier said.

We cruised around a little so I could get some pictures of the Binion longhorns. Half of the bulls are pure longhorn, and impressive-looking beasts they are.

Back at the ranchhouse, Sevier and the others told me how much they like being cowboys on the Binion ranch. Clayton Phipps, who grew up on his family's ranch not far away, said, "I love every day out here." The others agreed. Still, being a cowboy on somebody else's ranch is not an end to itself. All of the men said they wanted to have their own places some day, though they weren't sure how this could be accomplished. "If I don't, I'll die trying," Sevier said.

These days, Sevier said, it is difficult to find a man capable and willing to do all the types of work that need doing on the Binion ranch. He said a man who could do the work would deserve a top salary. "I'd probably pay him a thousand dollars a month," he said. "That's more than even a lot of married men make." That includes room and board of course.

DANIEL N. VICHOREK

Jim McCaskey

Jim McCaskey

I found Jim McCaskey on the street in Miles City during the Bucking Horse Sale in 1993. I saw by his outfit that he was a cowboy. He was minding his own business, not bothering anybody. He looked the way lonesome young women in cold-hearted big cities think a cowboy should look. I did a man-in-the-street interview.

Jim said he was twenty-nine years old, from Wibaux, and had worked as a cowboy ever since he was old enough to get into the bars. When he was younger, he rode some bareback horses and bulls, but has given that up. "By the time you're twenty-eight or twenty-nine you'll be out of the buckaroo stage," he said.

I asked him what there is about cowboying that keeps him doing it. "It's hard to explain. You feel it when you hit a ridgetop just at sun-up as the world comes alive. You feel it in the spring after a long cold winter when you finally see some blades of green grass and you know you've made it for another year. And there's tradition. My dad and granddad ranched, and it feels good to do the same thing.

"The basic values haven't changed. If it gets tough and cold, do it anyway. Too many things count on you to do your job. There aren't any personnel evaluations on the ranch, but your neighbors take care of that; they know if you're a good hand or not. The money's not much, but money is not everything anyway. Out there, you can sleep at night. The life is easygoing. You can take people at their face value."

He said the cowboy image is something that lots of people want to tap into. Every big city all over the country has a country western club where people go so show off their cowboy clothes, he pointed out.

I asked him what he'll be doing ten years from now. "Same thing I'm doing now. Except I'll probably have a wife and kids by then."

Jim left me with instructions. "Tell people we're still doin' it out here the way it should be done."

Martin Hedoesit

DANIEL N. VICHOREK

Martin Hedoesit is a young man who gave up the full-time cowboy life to raise a family. He has three kids now, but he still keeps his cowboy bed rolled up and ready to go. Martin, thirty-nine years old when I talked to him in 1993, was born at Crow Agency on Montana's Crow Indian Reservation. His father, Raphael, put in some time as a cowboy, and there was always somebody with boots and spurs around. "Cowboy was all I ever wanted to be," Martin said. "I was a-scared of Indians."

When he was a teen-ager, Martin liked to go to nearby ranches to help with branding and other chores. Sometimes he even skipped school to participate in such fun. His family didn't mind too much, he said, as long as he stayed out of trouble. He was a big kid, though, and when he was fifteen he could get served in the bars. Martin was still a teenager when he started hiring out on some of the big ranches near his home on Soap Creek, south of Hardin. He was not the only kid to hire out, but he liked it better than the others did. "The other kids were homesick," he said. "I never was. I was having the time of my life."

Those days, he lived a lot like a regular old-time cowboy. "Everything you had was in your bed," he said. "Bed was a piece of canvas, seventeen feet long and seven feet wide with snaps on it. You could put anything in there: sleeping bag, blankets, whatever you had, and your clothes. It rolls up into a roll about eighteen inches in diameter and four feet long. You get where you're going, unroll it, and there's home." A bed is a useful thing to have, and Martin keeps his rolled up and ready to go, in case he needs it. I asked Martin about his apprenticeship as a cowboy. "Old-timers told me, 'You gotta hire out tough.' My dad told me, 'If somebody chews your ass, it's because they like you.' They liked me a lot." He said there was a lot to be learned: cowboy etiquette, what to not do, and introduction to cow psychology. As an example of cowboy etiquette, he said, you learn never to ride in front of anybody, even if you have to ride way back around the herd to avoid it. Cow psychology: well, you can't make a cow go faster than she wants to go. Moving a cow takes however long it takes, and that's how long it takes. Hedoesit was an "A" student in cowboy studies, according to Ray Krone, owner of the nearby Soap Creek Ranch and one of Hedoesit's employers and professors.

I asked Hedoesit what there was about the cowboy life that he found so satisfying. A lot, he said. He gave me an example. "You go out to gather cattle in the early morning. The air is clean and frosty and nothing makes a sound. It comes daybreak and your horse snorts and wheezes a little, maybe clinks a rock with a shoe. Way out there somewhere you can hear a cow bellering. It just feels so good to be out there. But some of those days get to be a little long, too." He said people ask him, "Why do you live way out here?" and the only thing he knows about them is that they aren't very happy with themselves.

Despite his satisfaction with the cowboy life, Hedoesit gave up cowboying at one point and went to work in a nearby oil field as a roughneck. Working in the oil field gave him a whole new perspective on cowboying. A lot of his time on the oil-field job was spent working with cold iron. "You look at a piece of iron," he said. "Iron is cold and hard and it never gets tired or wears out. It's not like a horse or a man." One day as Martin was out in the oil field pondering the shortcomings of iron, a neighboring rancher, John Hammett, drove by. Hammett stopped and Hedoesit got in with him. Hammett hired him to work on his ranch, and that was the last of his work with cold iron. "I went from three thousand dollars a month to five hundred and fifty and I was the happiest son of a bitch alive," he said. For that matter, he still is outwardly about the happiest person you could ever meet. John Hammett's wife Mary had told me earlier that

Way out there somewhere you can hear a cow bellering. It just feels so good to be out there.

Facing page: Martin Hedoesit.

DANIEL N. VICHOREK PHOTOS

Above: Barrel racer and rodeo queen Billie Rose Hedoesit. Top: David Hedoesit—permanentaly atop his mount?

Hedoesit "makes everything easy," and I soon saw what she meant. Besides being continually cheerful, he's big enough to work as a front-end loader. "I use him as a windbreak, get behind him to stay out of the weather," John Hammett said.

Nowadays, Hedoesit still helps out John Hammett and other neighbors, but mainly he divides his time between working on his own place and a summer job as a maintenance worker for the National Park Service at the Bighorn Canyon National Recreation Area at Fort C.F. Smith.

"The Park Service job is really boring," he said, "but it puts some money in the pocket." And once in a while he has a little fun. Part of his job is doing campground maintenance in the Bighorn Canyon, which he and the other men reach by boat. Wherever there are campgrounds, there are bears, and this has led to entertainment.

One thing every cowboy wants to do is rope a bear, and one day Hedoesit had his chance. "All the other guys were sayin', 'Let's do it, let's rope 'im,' but I noticed once I got the rope on him I was all by myself," he said. He was going to put the bear into the ladies' room, but that didn't work out.

I asked Martin how you let a bear go, once you rope him. "Oh, they turn themselves loose," he said. He said it was okay to write about his bear roping because he already got into trouble over it.

When he's not working for the government or helping the neighbors, Martin works on his own place. It's just a little place, he said: 4,000 acres with fewer than 100 cows. His livestock also includes a few head of roping stock. Martin likes to go to rodeos to compete in the team roping. There's the chance to make a little money, but mostly it's just fun.

Just what is there about roping that is so much fun? I asked.

"It's like fly-fishing, or golf. Or maybe it's like when your wife goes shopping and she looks at every pair of socks in the store and then buys the first pair she looked at." I gathered that it is an art form that cannot be appreciated by persons without the proper cultivation and schooling.

"Guns go off, ropes go on," Martin said conclusively. I don't know what that means.

In order to rope a steer, Hedoesit said, you have to get in time with him, catch his rhythm. Roping at rodeos provides an adrenaline fix, he said. "You can hear your heart pounding in your ears. It's just like the bronc riders. It's a disease."

He said the roping disease is available to anybody who wants to get trained. Various schools provide the training, and a student of roping is better off if he starts with no experience rather than with a bunch of bad habits to overcome.

However, in the case of roping—as with other things—education needs to be well-rounded. Martin told of a farm boy who went to roping school and became a crackerjack roper, but the home team could still beat him because he didn't know how to ride.

Martin stays close to home and doesn't go to rodeos that he can't get to in a day. One limitation on his rodeoing is his daughter, Billie Rose, who was thirteen and more serious about rodeoing than her father. "She doesn't party or do anything other kids do," Martin said. "Horses are all she's interested in." Her 1993 winnings in barrel racing and "pole bending" were about $2,000, Martin said. "Of course, it cost us $1,500 to get the $2,000." Billie Rose fulfilled a big rodeo ambition in 1993, when she was selected queen of a kids' rodeo in Broadus. "That's all she's wanted to do since she learned to talk," Martin said, "be a barrel-racer and a rodeo queen."

Martin said Billie Rose's rodeo horse is probably worth $5,000 or maybe even $10,000. "We didn't pay anything for him. We just made him," he said. When I visited the Hedoesit Ranch, Billie Rose was standing in a cold barn combing an enormous gob of burrs out of her horse's tail. She seemed to be enjoying life just as much as Martin does.

Martin's son Skeeter, on the other hand, was ten and not interested in horses. "He has the TV disease," Martin said. Though Skeeter is a prize-winning Amateur Athletic Union wrestler. The youngest Hedoesit, David, was three when I visited, and the only time I saw him he was entertaining himself riding a large horse around the Hedoesit corral. It appeared to be about three David-lengths from the top of the horse to the ground, but David was not intimidated. He occasionally stopped the horse by a barrel and attempted to get off. He couldn't quite reach the top of the barrel. He lowered himself carefully until his feet were three inches from the barrel, but he couldn't see how far he had to go. Holding on to the saddle, he stretched as far as he could but still couldn't touch bottom. He got worried and hauled himself back up to ride some more. The horse stood patiently for all this. "When he gets bigger and starts to annoy the horse, he'll just buck him off," Martin said.

Getting bucked off is just a fact of life on a ranch, he said. He mentioned that his daughter Billie Rose had been bucked off hard not long before, went over the horse's head and landed on her back so hard that both heels broke off her new boots.

I asked Martin what he requires in a horse for his own use. "For one thing, he's gotta be able to carry me," he said. "With me and a saddle, it comes to about three hundred and forty pounds." The saddle weighs about forty pounds. Reflecting on his size reminded Martin of another thing he likes about working on ranches. "They know how to feed you." He reminisced happily over world-class apple pies and peach cobblers that he had seen come out of old wood stoves.

I asked Martin what he sees for the future of his ranch and himself. He said he wasn't sure. Before long, Billie Rose will be able to drive herself around to rodeos, and then he can go to different ones to rope, and maybe take that a little more seriously, he said. Maybe he'll get a little better grade of cattle on his place. "I don't know for sure. I operate on my own money. I'm too lazy to owe money; I don't want to be supporting the banker."

He takes a skeptical view of the modernization he sees on other ranches. "It used to be if you needed to dig a post hole you just used a bar and shovel," he said. "Now you've got three guys and a tractor."

Martin owns a tractor but doesn't use it to dig post holes. The only thing he does use it for is to groom the arena where he and friends practice their roping. "I'm no farmer," he said.

Eventually, he said, his kids will be out of college. Maybe then it will be time to gather up his cowboy bed and look for a job.

Getting bucked off is just a fact of life on a ranch.

MICHAEL S. CRUMMETT

MICHAEL S. CRUMMETT

Above: Silhouettes in the night.
Right: Cowboys don't mind a little fancy. Even if you get bucked off, you should look good doing it.
Far right: Barn geometry near Lavina.

Facing page: A serious drink after serious work.

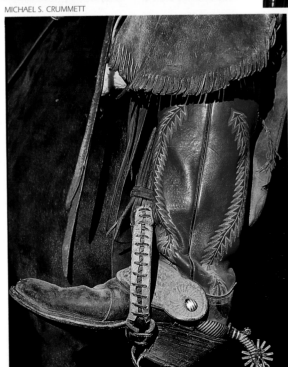

BOB ZELLAR/J-R AGENCY

Gator Ropes

In the process of researching this book, I cornered Marty Hedoesit and made him try to explain the favorite cowboy sport of roping. He made a heroic effort but had little success in getting through to me on this topic. He suggested that my education could benefit from a visit to the people at Gator Ropes in Helena. Considering that I live in Helena, he was amazed that I had never heard of Gator Ropes. But I have now.

Gator Ropes is a seven-year-old company that makes top-of-the-line ropes for rodeo steer ropers. The business is owned and operated by Judy Wagner and her husband Alvin. I visited Judy at the rope factory.

She said she wasn't looking for a job when she got into the rope business. Her husband is a sales representative for various types of Western gear, and someone suggested to him that Judy might want to go into business. She agreed, although it was not immediately clear what the business was.

The nature of the business became clear presently, and they called it Gator Ropes because the first rope they produced was green. For two years, Gator Ropes was headquartered in the Wagners' basement, but in the years since it has been in a steel building on North Montana Avenue. "We have no salesmen, and we are ninety percent wholesale," Judy said. Gator ropes are sold through Western stores in Montana and other states where cowboys need ropes, not to mention Canada.

The ropes begin as blank cords from a manufacturing plant, and Gator employees turn them into ropes that are almost ready for the rodeo. The blanks are made either of nylon or a nylon-polypropylene blend. Gator employees tie knots at the ends: the little eye loop, called a hondo, in one end, and a plain end knot in the other.

Judy said the proper tying of the hondos is critical to the function of the rope. If the hondo is turned even slightly from its proper

Judy Wagner with inventory of Gator Ropes.

DANIEL N. VICHOREK

angle, the rope will be difficult or impossible to use well. The hondo is protected from the rope sliding though it by a piece of rawhide called a burner. Gator ropes have a white rawhide burner that is a sort of trademark.

The ropes turned out by Gator come with numerous variations to suit the individual user. Variations include weight, length, diameter, stiffness, durability and color. Dying a rope adds weight and increases durability, Judy said. She said dyed ropes last longer than undyed for the same mysterious reason that blue jeans do not last as long as black ones. The stronger the dye concentration, the greater the durability. Various Gator ropes come in different colors. The Intimigator, for example, is aqua blue. The Instigator is cranberry red.

In team roping competition, one roper catches the head, the other the back feet of the steer. The rope for catching the head is shorter and softer, the one for the feet longer and harder. Gator ropes for each purpose come in four degrees of hardness. The 36-foot heel ropes come in medium soft, medium, medium hard, and hard. The 32-foot head ropes come in extra soft, soft, medium soft, and medium.

Judy said hardness and other rope characteristics in a rope are a matter of personal preference and ability. Gator produces seven different models of ropes for adults, each available in 32- and 36-foot lengths. They are available in diameters from slightly less than $3/8$ inch to $7/16$. Gator also makes two different ropes for kids.

Judy explained that a rope is an essential part of a rodeo cowboy's tool kit, along with his horse and saddle. As such, it requires special care. For example, she said a new rope should be broken in by using it to rope eight or ten steers, and then coiled loosely and put away overnight.

This break-in will stretch the rope and break down fibers in the core, she said, but not too much. Left overnight, the rope will relax, as Judy said, into its "true home," less tightly spun than when new. However, should one lose one's head and rope twenty steers with a new rope, it might stretch the rope too far, causing soft spots and lost durability. Even with the best care, a rope loses its usefulness for competitive roping sooner or later. "They get fuzzy," Judy said, which makes them slower to throw, and less able to slide though the hands.

None of this has much to do with ranch cowboys, Judy said. "A ranch cowboy can use a rope forever."

Judy said that rope making, and roping, are on the upswing. One new wrinkle in roping is handicap roping, which works like handicap golf, so that less skillful ropers can compete with more skillful ones. "This is getting real popular," she said.

Gator ropes are only for roping steers. Calf ropers use an entirely different sort of rope, of a type not made by Gator.

Steer ropers playing hard at Crow Fair rodeo.

A Montana Cowboy Album

DIANE ENSIGN

Right: Cowboy kitchen on the range.
Below: After the blizzard, a feast of mineral cake.
Far right: Alan Doane horseshoeing.

Facing page: Moving stock into the Gallatin Valley, near Logan, for the winter.

MICHAEL S. CRUMMETT

MICHAEL S. CRUMMETT

WILL BREWSTER

Above: Brahma bull rider just ready for his exit at the Miles City Bucking Horse Sale.
Left: After the ride during night-time competition, Billings.

MICHAEL S. CRUMMETT

Right: Hobbling his horse.
Below: Cleaning up, and reassuring, a wary newborn.
Far right: Rodeo stock on call.

Facing page: Wranglers take off after horses bolting from the herd.

BERT GILDART

BOB ZELLAR/J-R AGENCY

Those Tooke Horses

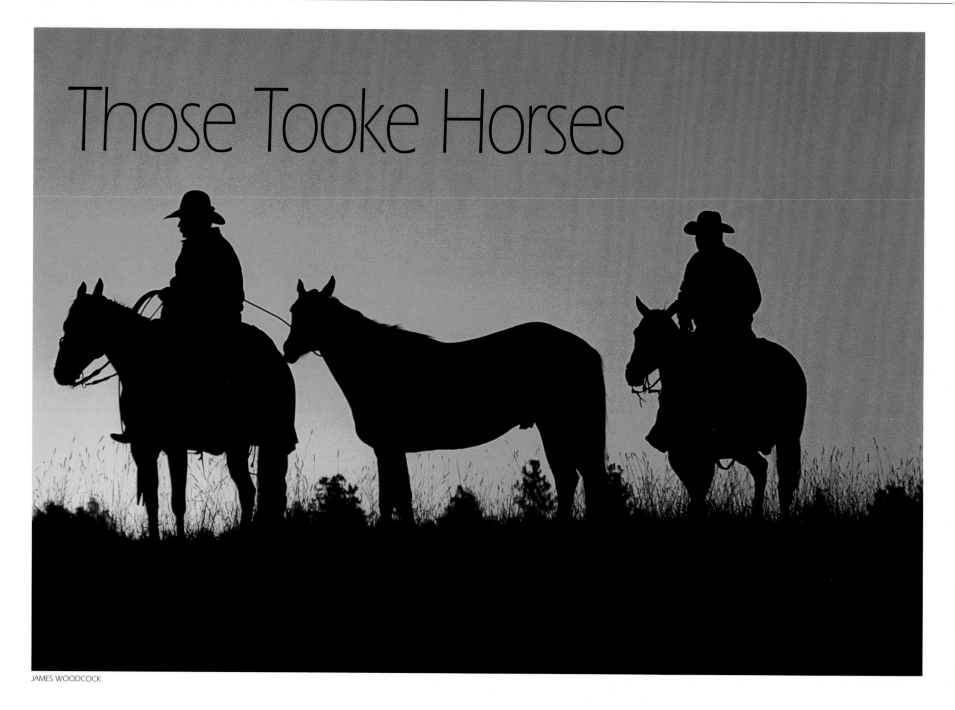

JAMES WOODCOCK

Whenever the senior generation of Montana's ranch and rodeo people get together, sooner or later the conversation turns to those famously rank Tooke horses that grow near Ekalaka, and the legendary founder of this foul brood, Feek Tooke. Mr. Tooke was one of six roughneck Irish brothers brought up on a homestead west of Ekalaka. His folks named him "Chandler Earl" but this became unwieldy while he was still a toddler and they tried calling him "Felix." His brother Fay, only a little older than Felix, had trouble saying "Felix," which always came out "Feek."

Ernest Tooke, son of Feek, was operating the family ranch when I visited in 1993, and had many recollections about his father and uncles. From the beginning, he said, they did not go gently. "It's a good thing Gramma was a nurse so she could keep them patched up," he said.

Being homesteaders on a tough land in tough times, the Tookes didn't have a lot of factory-made entertainment, but they did have livestock. Even the sweet-natured family milk cow, named Pulse after the man they bought her from, did a turn as a bucking cow. Pulse, it was said, was as gentle as the day was long, had a strong maternal instinct, and always gave two steaming buckets of milk every day. The boys couldn't leave her alone, though, and one day one of them just had to jump on her back out in the milking shed. This rider hit the roof hard, and Pulse's reputation as a wild bucking cow was launched. Pulse developed a long run of victories over various riders, with no losses. Feek's brother Red said he could ride her for sure, but three jumps out, Pulse threw Red like a javelin. After an impressive flight, Red hit the fence and became suspended when his head wedged between corral poles. Bystanders had to prize him out, once they quit laughing.

A less friendly cow was an ornery Hereford that somehow wound up at one of the rodeos that the Tookes put on at their ranch. The cowboy who was scheduled to ride this cow took one look at the mood she was in and disqualified himself. This presented an opportunity to Feek's brother Dick, who had a big crush on one of the local cowgirls but couldn't seem to make any headway. He needed to make a heroic show. He said he'd ride that cow.

The cow came out fast with Uncle Dick aboard, but not for long. She threw him off the front over her horns and began mauling him on the ground. Presently Dick got on his feet and started to run, but the cow followed closely, hooking him with her horns every other step. Dick hollered and screamed with each hooking. The race proceeded to the opposite side of the arena where Dick finally escaped over the fence, bleeding and with half his clothes torn off. The object of his affection was not moved to sympathy and nearly fell off the fence laughing, according to recollection.

The Tooke boys reached young adulthood in the 1920s and '30s, which was a sort of golden age for horses in eastern Montana. The whole country had filled up with homesteaders in the period between 1900 and 1920, but then times got too tough and the homesteaders pulled out. Many of them left their horses behind, especially their spoiled or mean horses, and for many years afterwards thousands of unclaimed horses of every description ran wild in the big empty country. Ernest Tooke said Feek built up the family ranch by catching these wild horses and selling them. From a small start, the ranch grew up to thirty-six square miles.

If the Tooke boys wanted to put on a rodeo, they could go out on the prairie and catch a good supply of untamed horses in a short period of time. And they often did. On the open sagebrush prairie some distance from where the buildings on the Tooke ranch are today, Ernest Tooke showed me the spot where some of these impromptu rodeos took place. These contests bore little resemblance to a modern rodeo—there was a corral of sorts where the outlaw horses were stored until they were needed, but there were no chutes, no announcer, not even

The speeding bronc had a good head of steam by the time he reached this edge of the world, having run a mile or so.

any prize money. The Tookes and their neighbor boys came to ride just for the fun of it.

One of the best remembered rides of those open country rodeos resulted not from a particularly noble horse, nor a brave effort by a cowboy, but from a sort of miscarriage of technology, if that's what it was. This ride may have had its roots during some long winter night, or some endless dusty afternoon when the cowboys were loafing around with nothing to do and launched perilously into creative thought. Idle hands were the devil's workshop, as usual. The cowboys decided to invent the "buck-off–proof saddle."

They took the seat off an old plow and fastened a portion of steel rim from a wagon wheel across the front as the fork of the saddle. The rider "sort of screwed himself in," fitting his legs through the small spaces between the seat and the wagon rim. They completed the invention by attaching it to a saddle tree with stirrups and a cinch. They called it "the beartrap."

Once installed in the beartrap, no rider was going to be bucked off, at least not in one piece. Ernest Tooke suggests that the inventors and users of this contraption were influenced by the supply of sharp-edged whiskey manufactured by some of the remaining homesteaders. Their imaginations only got as far as thinking about themselves being able to ride anything. They stopped short of imagining what would happen if a horse fell, for example.

At any rate, on that well-remembered rodeo day on the Tooke ranch, one of the local hearties rode a horse with the beartrap, and everything went fine until the pick-up man came to catch the horse. The bucking horse's halter was pulled off accidentally, and the horse, suddenly uncontrolled and with his rider trapped in the beartrap, took off to the west where he knew a horse could be free and safe.

The rolling country where the Tooke ranch is located is a sort of world to itself and, like old-style worlds, it has an abrupt edge on the western side. This edge is the divide where the land suddenly breaks at a sharp angle and drops down into the Powder River badlands. In some places the break is almost vertical, with a drop of several hundred feet. The speeding bronc had a good head of steam by the time he reached this edge of the world, having run a mile or so. At the last possible second, just as horse and rider were set to become airborne, the pick-up man, full of adrenaline and capable of superhuman feats, launched a long throw with his rope and succeeded in snatching horse and rider back from the verge of messy destiny.

In 1931, the Tooke brothers built a regular rodeo arena at the family ranch, complete with bucking chutes. The Tooke rodeos became popular entertainment, with riders and spectators coming from miles around. By the mid-1930s, the supply of suitable bucking horses began to dry up. The federal government decided that too many unclaimed horses were eating up the range, so all the free ones out on the range were rounded up and sold, mostly as dog food for $2 to $5 apiece.

Feek Tooke considered the future and concluded that bucking horses were going to be in short supply. He decided to design his own line of bucking horses to meet this far-off need. He was the first, or at least one of the first, to believe that bucking qualities could be bred into a horse. He took plenty of heckling from people who thought it could not be done. They told him he was crazy.

When Feek decided to try to breed bucking horses, the material he needed was not far away. One of Feek's friends had an albino Arabian stud with a serious attitude problem. He hated humanity with an intense passion, according to Ernest Tooke. This horse, named Snowflake, "was the meanest horse I ever laid eyes on," Ernest Tooke said. Snowflake would not permit a human on foot in a corral where he was, and had to be thrown to get a halter on or off. Snowflake had the capacity to pass on his temperament—he was always breaking in with the neighbors' mares and the offspring were outlaws just like him, greatly annoying the neighbors. The more Feek Tooke saw of the albino, the more he thought he had found the start of his bucking string. He already had some mares that were pretty good buckers, and when he purchased Snowflake in 1944 or 1945 and put him in with these mares, the result was impressive. Snowflake's offspring, Ernest Tooke said, were "beautifully marked glass-eyed pintos," and each of them liked humanity just as much as their dad did.

The story of the Tooke horse genesis has two parts— one part consisting of Feek Tooke's careful consideration in selecting the incredibly rank albino stud—and the other part pure luck. The luck part began in 1943 when Tooke decided to raise draft horses. Kicking off this enterprise, Feek bought a registered Shire stallion from a horse farm in Iowa. This horse was named King Larego, and weiged 2,000 pounds when he was two years old. He had won a blue ribbon at the Iowa State Fair. His task in Montana was to sire work horses that would be gentle and placid but with the strength of Hercules.

The plans for King Larego went haywire. First, he was injured and ruined as a stud after he had sired only one colt. Second, that one colt, named Prince, though outwardly identical to his father, had the same disposition as Snowflake. Some people opined that there was something weird out on the Tooke Ranch. Maybe something in the grass, they suggested. Or maybe some sort of nightmare chemical was in that flavorful alkali water that springs up in the coulees out there above Powder River. After all, the Tooke boys themselves grew up drinking that water.

At any rate, Feek knew a good thing when he saw it. He crossbred the offspring of Prince and Snowflake and came up with the homicidal line of Roman-nosed, plate-footed, feather-legged rodeo dynamite known for over forty years now as the Tooke horses.

"I wish," Ernest Tooke told me as we rode in his pickup on the Tooke ranch, "that I had the best 100 horses that ever ate grass out here. If I trucked them around to the rodeos, the cowboys would get in their pickups and leave." He estimates that the Tooke breeding line has produced more than 4,000 horses over the years. A lot of rodeo stock producers have horses with the Tooke bloodline in them, and those horses and their descendants will be pounding cowboys into the ground long into the future. Many Tooke horses of the past are in the record books, and many others will last in memory until the passing of the last of the old riders.

There was, for example, the horse named General Custer. Custer was the son of Prince, and weighed 1,800 pounds. He was eighteen hands high, which brought the top of his back just about level with the top of an ordinary bucking chute. The rest of him filled the chute as though poured in. As Ernest said, the sight of him was enough to start a poor cowboy's knees to knocking.

Despite his enormous proportion, General Custer was said to be as agile as a cat, capable of standing on his forelegs and kicking nearly straight up, and his shoulders delivered shocks like piston rods. Something about the weight of a horse increases the pain of the ride. Imagine making a parachute jump with cannonballs tied to your feet. Then imagine falling out of the sky while tied to 1,800 pounds of horse meat.

Ernest said the General was just about impossible to ride. He recalled the spring of 1962 when Custer was taken away from his brood mares to perform in a rodeo at Miles City. Deprivation of the mares in the spring was enough to aggravate the General, who bore a hereditary short fuse anyway. Besides which he was in terrific shape, shiny from eating grain, and mentally keyed up. Poor Alvin Nelson, the world champion who got on the General in Miles City that day, had a short ride with a hard landing.

And General Custer begat Major Reno. The Major was not as big as his dad, but equaled him in disposition and probably surpassed him in difficulty, according to Ernest Tooke.

DANIEL N. VICHOREK

Valentine's hatred of humanity was so pronounced that he could not express it adequately without using his teeth.

Some Tooks horses on the range. "Old stud" in foreground.

Cut to the National Finals Rodeo (NFR), 1968. Larry Mahan, called "Goldfinger" by some rodeo people because he was the first to win more than $50,000 in a season, twice All-Around World Champion, approached the end of the saddle bronc event with only one other man still in competition. The other man was bucked off one of his horses, and Mahan rode all of his until there was only one left. Ride that one and he would be the champion. This last horse was Major Reno, said to be "big headed, Roman-nosed." Starting flat-footed, the Major could jump a six-foot fence. In an earlier performance in 1968, he jumped out of a seven-foot rodeo arena after launching his rider into a low orbit. Mahan lasted four jumps.

The next year, Mahan drew Major Reno as his first horse at the NFR. Mahan successfully rode all of his other horses in the finals that year but he didn't ride Major Reno. In the years 1967 through 1969, Mahan hit the ground only twice at the Finals: Major Reno both times.

Over the years the Tooke horses have won major awards. Between 1967 and 1993, 12 Tooke horses won seventeen major bucking horse championship awards. Up to 1993, Tooke horses won seven National Finals Rodeo Best Saddle Bronc awards. A horse named Bobby Joe, grandson of General Custer, won in 1991, 1992, and 1993. These awards are granted on the basis of voting by the top ten rodeo riders, and rodeo people equate them to winning the Kentucky Derby.

Some Tooke horses never won anything but will never be forgotten anyway. Take the horse called Valentine, for example. Valentine's hatred of humanity was so pronounced that he could not express it adequately without using his teeth. As Ernest Tooke said, he was "vicious as a wildcat," and he'd blast suddenly out of a herd of horses with his mouth open like a baboon and his long teeth ready to punish any human he could get to.

When they put Valentine in the bucking chute, he'd reach up and bite everybody around, all the guys with their flesh hanging over the edge of the chute yowling and scrambling off. Once in the arena, he'd bite his rider if he could, and when the pick-up man came alongside he'd bite him too. The pick-up men wore chaps to protect their legs, but Valentine learned how to get his nose under the chaps and inflict big ugly horse-bite bruises on their pale thighs.

After a while Feek decided that Valentine should wear a muzzle when he bucked, to impede his man-eating tendencies, and so he became the horse in the iron mask. Sitting around Miles City listening to old timers, I heard about when Feek included Valentine in a contingent of horses to be ridden by college students. Someone took issue at this and asked Feek if he didn't think Valentine was a little rough for young kids. According to the old-timers' memory, Feek then said, "Maybe they'll decide to go into a different line of work."

"You had to know Feek," the old-timers said, lest this greenhorn think ill of him. Everybody said it. Much affection was attached to him. Something to do with being an Irishman.

Despite his accomplishments, Feek Tooke could not do everything. Take flying for example. At one point Feek and his brother Fay decided to become flying cowboys and signed up for flight lessons. Feek thought an airplane would be dandy for chasing his bucking horses out of the Powder River badlands where they were inclined to hide and give the slip to any riders coming in after them. Feek's lessons lasted until one day when he decided to use part of his air time to chase horses. It became clear to the instructor that Feek was going to fly right into the ground, so he washed him out of pilot training. "A menace," the instructor said Feek was. Fay lasted a little longer but not much. On a flight to Lewistown one day, the instructor became drowsy and asked Fay to take the controls while the instructor took a little nap. He woke up sometime later to find the aircraft banking in big lazy circles with Fay asleep at the controls. That was the end of flying for another Tooke.

"That would not be a good horse for an ordinary person to try to ride."

The next generation of Tookes had better luck with aviation. Ernest uses a Super Cub to commute the twenty miles between the Tooke ranch and Ekalaka, where he and his wife have a home and spend part of their time. The day I appeared on the scene, Ernest took me out to the ranch from Ekalaka in his pickup. It was a fine November day in Montana, crisp and cool. In late afternoon the sun was a weak red ball off to the southwest, looking every bit of 93 million miles away. The red light gave a crimson cast to the grass and the sage. It had snowed the day before, and thin little drifts, glacial blue against the red, an inch or so deep and three or four wide, snaked along on bare ground where the brush had gathered them at the edge of clearings.

We were looking for the Tooke horses, following ranch roads that wandered here and there. Antelope squirted out of coulees ahead of us, not much alarmed, casting long shadows. Ernest pointed at a thatch of brush on the distant horizon, identifying the spot as the site of the original Tooke homestead where the six wild Irishmen had their boyhoods.

Presently we found the horses, first one small bunch and then another. At first glance, they did not seem remarkable in appearance. Then, however, one of the bunches ran off a little, and a hierarchy became apparent. A muscular bay horse with a long tail and matted mane moved off to one side and struck a proprietary pose. A couple of smaller horses held back from the main bunch, steering clear of the bay.

The bay, Ernest said, is the "old stud," who has no other name, though he is a grandson of the famous General Custer. The smaller horses keeping their distance were the "young studs." Ernest said the old stud has never been in a corral, never had a halter on, never been subjected to any handling. He had been, for all practical purposes, a wild horse all his life, born on the range, lived there all his life, seventeen years by then, and probably would die there.

I got out of the truck to take pictures and the old stud came toward me, though rather placidly. Still, I remembered the horse in the iron mask and got back into the truck. Ernest said the old stud is not a meat-eater, however, and was merely hoping I had a cookie for him.

Ernest pointed out a young horse in the bunch as a good example of a Tooke horse. Not yet a year old, this horse was already the size of an ordinary saddle horse, heavily built, feet coming to the size of skillets, a red and white pinto with a white face, outsized head and big Roman nose, and at least one glassy eye. Something was there of the original man-eating Arabian, and the renegade son of King Larego too. "That would not be a good horse for an ordinary person to try to ride," Ernest told me.

These days, the Tooke ranch is a cattle operation with a few bucking horses left to themselves out on the range to reproduce. "We sell maybe twenty a year now," Ernest said.

For his part, Feek Tooke had the satisfaction of proving that orneriness and bucking skills were hereditary traits. In 1968, Feek appeared at the National Finals Rodeo to accept awards for two of his horses that were voted outstanding the previous year—Sheep Mountain as best saddle bronc, and Bay Meggs as second best bareback bronc. Sitting a fine palomino, Feek accepted the awards and rode out of the arena. After dismounting behind the chutes, had a heart attack and died. They found him still clutching his awards. He was fifty-nine years old.

When they talk about Feek, his son and all those who knew him, "and you had to know him," they agree of course that he died too young. Still, they take comfort in knowing that he went out the way he would have wanted, with his boots on like a true son of the West, and having proved that the idea he believed in was right.

"Giving the bronco a slicker lesson" was photographer L.A. Huffman's title for this 1904 image.

MICHAEL S. CRUMMETT

Above: Breakfast is on.
Left: Just wait 'til it's my turn!

Facing page: Cattle drive takes the right of way.

John
Hammett

DANIEL N. VICHOREK

Two cowboys named John Hammett have plied their trade in what used to be the wide open country at the foot of the Bighorns and Pryors south of Hardin. John Hammett senior arrived in the north country from Texas in the late 1880s or early '90s. He was never definite about the time and circumstances of his arrival. "He had an original story for everybody," said the present John Hammett, son of the original. The profession of the senior Hammett was "cowpuncher," according to his son.

The cowboy I am talking about here is John Hammett Jr., who was born in Wyoming in 1926. Two years later the Hammetts moved to the Bighorn country of Montana, where John senior worked for one of the big operators, E.L. Dana, owner of the Birdhead Ranch. John came of age in the latter days of the old open-range era. Starting when he was fourteen, he rode with his father in the summers, and went to school the rest of the year. When he was seventeen, he joined the Navy. The Navy was his choice, he said, because that was the only branch you could go into if you were seventeen.

When he returned to cow country in 1946, it was a changed world. "Times had changed to beat hell," he said. "All the young guys got drafted, so the ranches had to use either old guys or young kids." To get by with fewer men, the ranches had fenced off a lot of range into pastures. They didn't have to put night guards on the cattle any more, no more nighthawks were needed to take care of the horses at night. The war also set the stage for the arrival of the four-wheel-drive vehicle, which, along with the horse trailer, caused major changes in cattle country.

Back from the war and finding things were done differently than before, John was at loose ends. "I tried a lot of things," he said. "I didn't accomplish much. I worked as a cowboy for five or six outfits. I wrangled dudes, guided some hunters, broke some horses." He worked in the Butte mines, roughnecked in an oil field. "I

didn't like any of it as a steady diet." He went to Texas one winter and worked for a cow outfit where they still used the roundup wagon. He thought it odd that the cook with the wagon used Dutch ovens. In Montana, they had a regular wood stove mounted in the wagon, with the bottom of the stove cut out so the ashes could fall out on the ground. They took the lids off when they were moving so they wouldn't flip off and get lost when the wagon hit a bump. Texas, he said, was mainly brush with a little grass. He understood why John Sr. left it, whenever he had.

Hammett worked in some rodeos, broke his back in one, broke his leg working on the Antler Ranch. After breaking his back, he took the cast off and won the amateur saddle-bronc riding in a rodeo. Back in those days, he said, a cowboy had a better chance of making money in a rodeo. They usually lasted three days, and each rider got a horse every day, rather than one horse per rodeo as is sometimes done today. It was harder to get to the rodeos; roads were not so good, and vehicles were slow.

One rodeo event that John was good at was the wild horse race. Rarely performed these days, the wild horse race consisted of several teams of contestants, each with a bucking horse that they had to get saddled and ride around the track. In a rodeo at Red Lodge, John's team won two firsts and a second in the three days. One of the team members explained to a bystander, "At the Antler Ranch, we used to get a horse just like that all to ourselves every day."

Finally it came time to settle down, and John got married and settled on a little ranch on Rottengrass Creek east of Fort Smith. There he and his wife Mary raised sheep. They quit sheep finally because they had so much trouble with coyotes, and went back to raising cattle. In 1979 they leased the place where Mary grew up, on Soap Creek, where I visited them. They live by themselves now, their four daughters having grown up

Facing page: John and Mary Hammett.

MICHAEL S. CRUMMETT PHOTOS

Right and below: Working fashions.
Far right: Winter chores.

Facing page: Barrel racers get serious under the lights at Billings' night rodeo.

and left. "We made them into cowboys," John said. None of them went into the ranching business. "They all said, 'There's got to be an easier way to make a living'," Mary said.

Being married to a cowboy and living on a ranch is no bed of roses, Mary said. She said for most cowboys, "The only reason they got married was so they could get their clothes washed." Ranch work is not always a lot of fun either. "When it's snowing and blowing and you have to feed the calves and a heifer is trying to have a calf, it's not too shiny. Otherwise, it's the romance of the West," she said.

John and Mary are whimsical when they talk about the changes they have seen. "They call it progress," Mary said. "Everything has got modern. You'd have a terrible time now getting people to live like we did. We grew up in the Depression when you thought you were fine if you had anything, had a job, had something to put in your belly."

There is a certain satisfaction in having survived the tough times. It wasn't any fun at the time, certainly, but the experience of making it through is worth something. It is an experience not available to later generations. "It's good to have been here before things got modern," Mary said.

"Everything is all plowed up and fenced now. They don't do things the way they used to. But who has twenty-five thousand cattle now anyway?" At least two of the ranches in the vicinity had that many in the '30s.

Not that the Hammetts are opposed to progress. They bought a Thiokol snowcat to keep them from ever getting snowed in again. "This road up here can be a bear," Mary said.

Even the way of breaking horses has changed a lot. "It's more of a science now," John said. "It used to be, we wouldn't break horses until they were at least four years old, maybe eight. We'd rope 'em and take 'em down, tie up a hind foot and put a halter on 'em, then let 'em up. Then we'd sack 'em out." The term "sack 'em out" refers to the practice of flopping an old coat or a gunny sack at a horse to get them accustomed to movement and unexpected events, such as someone throwing a saddle blanket on their backs.

"They do more quicker with horses these days. They handle them from the time they are colts. It used to be if you could catch a horse and get a saddle on him, he was ready to go to work."

John and Mary said they sometimes think about retiring. I asked them what they would do if they were to retire. "Probably go nuts," John said. "But of course by then, we'll be so old we can just sit around in our wheelchairs." That might be a while. John Hammett Sr. lasted until he was, most people thought, a few months shy of 100 years old. Ray Krone said he had to be at least 120.

The present John Hammett said he doesn't have any major regrets about his life as a cowboy, though it has been difficult to follow some advice his father once gave him: "Never learn to run a tractor or build a fence."

"I think he was afraid I was going to turn into a farmer," John said.

Being married to a cowboy and living on a ranch is no bed of roses.

Morning comes early in eastern Montana. L.A. Huffman noted that these roundup outfits were on the move at 4:30 A.M.

GARRY WUNDERWALD

JAMES WOODCOCK

MICHAEL S. CRUMMETT

MICHAEL S. CRUMMETT

Above: Cooling off after a hard day's ride.
Left: Ranch home decor.
Far left: Quiet time.

Facing page: Gently moving.

Shelley Mackay and Babe Billingsley

Shelley Mackay

DANIEL N. VICHOREK

As I was searching in the eastern part of Montana for colorful 19th-century–style cowpokes that I could interview for this book, somebody said to me, "You ought to talk to Shelley Mackay. She could just as well live in the 19th century. She doesn't even care if she gets her mail."

I proceeded to track Ms. Mackay down and discovered it's not true that she is not at home in this century. It's just that this century is not that much different from the last one out where she lives, at least as the important things are concerned. Sitting in the kitchen of her new ranchhouse on Rattlesnake Creek, Shelley explained the local time warp. "This is livestock country, not farming country," she said. "This land hasn't changed in a hundred years and probably won't change much more." At least she hopes not.

Mackay came to the ranching business by choice, rather than inheritance. Born in Bozeman, she attended college in California, emerging with a biology degree. She tried some office work after graduation but found it only raised her blood pressure. Then in 1974 she had the chance to come and live with an aunt, Mary Billingsley (known unfailingly as "Babe"), on Billingsley's ranch south of Baker. That's where the two of them still are. And happily.

Enthusiasm fairly bursts out of Mackay when she talks about working on the ranch and the contrast between her and Babe and the poor devils who are trapped in conventional jobs in big cities. "My life is my hobby," Mackay said. "Some people hate to get up in the morning, hate to go to work." Unlike people who have to face the same horror show day after day, Mackay said, she gets up every morning with a wide choice of things that she can do that day. If she doesn't feel like doing one thing, she can do something else. An outsider might interpret that as meaning that there is so much work to do on a ranch that it can never be finished. But then an outsider would be without the "hidden optimism" that Mackay said is essential to keep ranchers working.

Working on a ranch clearly is a more cooperative effort than the average office job, Mackay said.

"Everything here works willingly. It's not a fight. It's a fun thing." By "everything," Mackay means that besides her and Babe, all the animals have their jobs too; chickens laying eggs, dogs helping with the cattle and running off varmints, horses carrying riders, and cows making beef. Though maybe the cows wouldn't be such hard workers if they understood the nature of their contribution to the beef production.

Working with animals is much different from doing paperwork or dealing with abstractions, Mackay said. "A lot of living things depend on you here. You can go out and talk to them." Working with animals also has its imperatives, things that have to be done no matter what. In the winter, for example, cattle have to be fed every day. Mackay recalled a day when her brother was visiting and a classic Montana blizzard whited out the world. Shelley put on her heavy clothes to go out and feed the cattle, and her brother, who lives in a southern state, said, quite horrified, "You're not going out there?" But of course she was. Cattle need even more feed in cold weather to keep their body temperatures up.

Shelley and Babe work the ranch alone, and I asked what happens if they get sick when essential things have to be done. "We don't get sick," Mackay said. "We get flu shots, but more than that it's a good cool breath of fresh air that keeps us healthy." Enthusiasm again. She said it's people like her brother who get sick, sitting in an office all day until pent-up adrenaline topples them.

Every so often, Mackay said, she leaves the ranch for a while and goes to other states to visit relatives. She enjoys her relatives but her time in the outside world gets to be an ordeal, she said. "I find myself wondering how things are going back at the ranch, how the sick calf is and stuff like that." She is like the ancient Chinese who never felt the need to explore the world because they already lived in the one place that was worth living in.

One benefit of living where she does, Mackay said, is

LARRY MAYER/BILLINGS GAZETTE

WILL BREWSTER

MICHAEL S. CRUMMETT

MICHAEL S. CRUMMETT PHOTOS

Above: Horses atop Big Horn Canyon.
Right: Beginning the fight.

Facing page, left: One horse likely bound for the rodeo circuit from the Miles City Bucking Horse Sale.
Right, top and bottom: Watching rodeo requires concentration.

With some imagination, the buttes looked like castles on the skyline.

that she is a member of a close-knit community. Not a single other house is visible from the house where Shelley and Babe live, and I asked Shelley what she meant by "community." After some thought, she said her community consists of the thirty or so people who inhabit the 900 square miles in her vicinity, east to the Dakota border. They all know each other of course, and get together for community efforts such as branding calves. "Forty or fifty people show up for branding," she said.

One difference between Mackay's community and the familiar urban community is the relationship among the generations, she said. "In the ranch community, older people are valued. All the generations normally live together. We get inspiration and common knowledge from our elders that we can't get from book-learnin'." For example, when foot rot threatens to become a problem, Babe whips up a concoction: a mixture of sheep dip, turpentine, and kerosene. "We don't need Terramycin," Shelley said.

But older people contribute much more than ideas on how to doctor sick critters. Shelley said Babe made her understand that material things are not the most important aspect of life. This teaching had a hard test. Not long ago, the old ranchhouse that Babe and Shelley were living in burned down. It happened at night and almost nothing was saved. One of the neighbors who came to the fire noted Mackay's calm in the face of total loss and told her, "If I didn't know you better I'd think you burned your own house."

Mackay said when her time comes she will be ready to assume her proper role as an elder in the community. Looking toward that time, Shelley and Babe have begun grooming a cousin of Shelley's to take over the ranch eventually. Shelley said they hope they can instill their values in her cousin. He also needs to understand a few realities, she said. "I'll tell him, 'You won't be rich, but you won't be in a soup line.' He'll need to be a frugal type."

Which does not mean you can't buy things you need. "We just save up," she said. At the time I interviewed them, they were in the market for a horse trailer. Prior to that, they saved up for a computer to do the taxes and keep track of livestock records.

To some people who live far away from the rural ranch scene, people who live for their vacations and time off and trips far away from it all, it may seem strange and even unsettling to hear Shelley Mackay say, "My life is my hobby." That, after all, is a slogan that could be stated proudly by any workaholic.

Workaholics are all around, and it is not difficult to ask them why they work. They never say that they do it for spiritual reasons. Mackay, on the other hand, does say this. "We're kind of laid back out here," she said. "We like to whistle and listen to the birds. It's a spiritual heritage."

This heritage runs back to the time before the land had its most recent change, which was the passing of the buffalo and their replacement with cattle. Direct evidence of the buffalo is fresh in memory on the ranch. Between some buttes just north of the ranch buildings, an abundance of buffalo bones littered the ground until they were hauled off and sold for fertilizer, Babe said. Whether the hunters were red or white, no one knows.

The ranch abounds in Indian artifacts, and someone from the National Geographic Society wanted to do an archaeological dig. "I told them, 'Let's leave the spirits alone'," Mackay said.

Shelley has a strong awareness that the land had earlier users. "Where my horse puts his foot, an Indian pony put his foot," she said.

Horses are the customary mode of transportation on the ranch. "We don't drive on the land. We like to get out and smell the brush." Getting out on the land also has its therapeutic value. "I like people, but I need time for myself," Shelley said. When she needs time, she saddles a horse, buckles on her side arm, and goes for a ride. She packs the heat primarily for porcupines, which are a serious hazard to cattle.

Despite the attractive elements of the ranch life that is available in her neighborhood, Mackay said she is not worried about any population explosions. "We don't see any Ted Turners out here. It's too harsh for most people. It gets to a hundred and twenty in the summer and forty below in the winter."

The biggest threat to the ranch way of life, Mackay said, comes not from the elements, but from legislation and regulations put into force by people with no knowledge of what they are dealing with. "Ranchers used to wear the white hats, and now we are suspected of causing all sorts of problems. We wear the black hats now."

She has a plan to help combat this problem. Basically, she wants to bring people out to her ranch to get some experience at ranch work, and get educated in the process. "A lot of people have a fantasy thing about ranches, and want to live it out. I figure we could bring out one or two people a week and let them see how we do things. We'd like to impress them with our feelings and knowledge. We'd like to show them that we are environmentally sound. I know part of the problem we have is that people envy what ranchers have, and they're afraid we are going to abuse the land."

She'd like to show them the wildlife—mule deer, peregrine falcons, burrowing owls, golden eagles. "We don't use any herbicides or pesticides. Maybe if people see what ranching is all about," she said, "we can at least start wearing gray hats." At present, hunters and some other outsiders, mostly from other states, come to the ranch. Shelley said these people usually have a great appreciation of the land. "Some of them are just mesmerized," she said. She shakes her head telling of one man who would not kill a porcupine though she had specifically told him to. "He said it would be a sacrilege," she said.

The idea of bringing city slickers out to work and observe on real ranches is not a new one. Several outfits are doing it in different ways in Montana, and Shelley has talked to some of them for pointers on how to go about accomplishing what she has in mind. "One problem they have is what to do about cellular phones," she said. "Some outfits let them keep them, some don't."

Food for dudes is another question. One outfitter told Shelley he caters primarily to CEOs of big corporations and they demand gourmet food. "I said, 'Whoa, mountain oysters [bull testicles] are about as close as I get to gourmet food'." Another possible problem is that dudes enjoy themselves so much that the same ones keep coming back year after year. This is at odds with Shelley's goal of educating as many people as she can. Despite all, cellular phones, gourmet food, and high recidivism, one suspects Shelley will accomplish her goal. "We're enthusiastic, optimistic, and we can deal with people," she said. "We'd like to share."

My talk with Shelley and Babe was all conducted at their kitchen table. As we talked we looked out a big window that faces north. Just outside the yard, a hay meadow slants up to a ridge and several buttes. Grass in the meadow was fawn-colored under the November overcast and the buttes rose up yellow against the sky. The coulee containing Rattlesnake Creek angled down from the far ridge, jogging gently this way and that on the meanderings that bring it past the ranchhouse. A growth of box elder and green ash followed the bottom of the coulee.

"I suppose it looks pretty bleak out there," Shelley said. I was still looking. With some imagination, the buttes looked like castles on the skyline. The bare branches of the box elder and green ash stood stark against the pale land like Japanese script down the side of a print. "Not really," I said. "Maybe in January though."

DANIEL N. VICHOREK

Sheila Kirkpatrick wearing and showing her creations.

Kirkpatrick Custom Hat Company

When the state of Montana was celebrating its centennial and wanted to send a commemorative cowboy hat to the president of the United States, it was not necessary to look out of state for the hat. The Kirkpatrick Custom Hat Company of Wisdom still aims to please the working cowboy with the hats it makes, but many of those hats eventually land on various celebrities. Sheila Kirkpatrick, the official hatter, named a few: Hank Williams Jr., Willard Scott, George Strait, Cheryl Ladd, Pea Eye in the *Lonesome Dove* sequel, not to mention the membership of a wild west club in Munich.

Sheila said celebrities have a big influence on hat styles. "A guy like George Strait," for example. People see his hat and want one like it." But of course hat styles change anyway. "In the Sixties and Seventies you had the real high crown, and now they're not so high," she said. "If you look back at the Fifties, hats were entirely different."

Sheila didn't start with the intention of catering to celebrities. When she was ten years old, she was already putting shape into hats with the steam from a teakettle. Later she worked for a custom hatter in Billings, and developed what she calls her "God-given talent—my only one" of making fine hats.

She wound up in Wisdom after marrying Buzz Kirkpatrick, a rancher from the vicinity, and opened the hat shop to pick up a little extra money. That was ten years before I visited the shop in 1994. "We started out like regular cowboys—broke," she said. They borrowed money to get the operation running, and word of mouth has kept them busy ever since. "We're beyond mom and pop now," Sheila said. At the time of my visit, five people were employed at least part of the time in the shop, turning out two or three hats a day, fifteen or twenty a week. Sheila said they might get up to ten a day sometime. "It's hard to improve productivity without sacrificing quality."

Quality is one of the hallmarks of Kirkpatrick hats, another being artistry. "We started with the cowboy in mind," Sheila said. "Cowboys use their hats for shade and protection. They had to be durable." For example, black dye in a Kirkpatrick hat does not run down the neck of the wearer caught in a rainstorm, Sheila said.

Besides quality, style is important to cowboys. A cowboy's hat and other personal gear are expressions of his personality, Sheila said. "Their hearts go into it. They will spend their last dime on a good saddle or pair of boots."

Keeping the cowboy in mind has influenced the price of the Kirkpatrick hats. "We try to stay no more than twenty or thirty dollars above factory-made hats," Sheila said, but noted that recent price increases for the factory hats have brought them in line with the Kirkpatrick products. "We try to keep them where a cowboy can afford them," she said.

Kirkpatrick hats come in three grades: 5X

for $160, 10X for $225, and 20X for $350. Sheila explained that the X rating is an old traditional method of rating felt. Specifically, it refers to the amount of beaver fur in it.

In the old days, Sheila said, it might have been that 5X was supposedly 50 percent beaver. All that she can promise these days, she said, is that 5X has some beaver in it, with the rest being rabbit. The soft inner fur of the beaver is better than any other fur for making felt, Sheila explained. The 10X hats have more beaver than the 5X, and the 20X is 100 percent beaver.

The felt is manufactured in St. Louis and formed into hat blanks, which is what the Kirkpatricks start with. These blanks look a little like the hats that Hoss Cartwright used to wear. Their brims are unfinished and the crowns are high and uncreased. Starting with a blank, Sheila can shape the felt into just about any kind or shape of felt hat, some of which no cowboy would ever get drunk enough to put on. Sheila said she has made fedoras suitable for Wall Street, derbies, and a fair number of Indiana Jones models. Hats on display in the shop cover a wide spectrum in color and style. Many are vividly colored, and some would look right at home at a yodeling festival in the Alps. Sheila said the weirdest hat she ever made was for a teddy bear.

Sheila showed me a cowgirl hat that she was proud of, with a black brim and red crown. Interlocking hearts were incised in the crown. She said she had taken it to a style show where it was enthusiastically received. "It's going to be popular," she said. Sheila's skill and artistry were recognized in 1992 when she was inducted into the Cowgirl Hall of Fame for her hat making.

The stylish cowgirl hat was an example of the direction Sheila said she wants to take her hat business—into the art world. Besides making the old standards for cowboys—the Montana crease, the rancher crease, the RCA (Rodeo Cowboys of America) crease—she wants to move into creating individual hats that are works of art. She has already moved some distance in this direction, and her hats have been displayed in several galleries. Along with the displays, Sheila gives talks on hat making, which she says hasn't changed all that much in the last hundred years. "We still use those same tools they used a hundred years ago," she said.

An example of the Kirkpatricks' flexibility is an idea they are considering to make cowboy hats with earflaps, for skiers. Back in the Sixties, the Olympic skier Billy Kidd wore his cowboy hat while skiing, and Sheila said she thinks there is a market for such hats.

While approaching the art world on one side, the Kirkpatricks will continue catering to their cowboy clientele on the other. "We're western raised," she said. "We represent cowboy interests."

When a cowboy's old friend—his hat—has reached an intolerable state, he can send it off to the Kirkpatrick Custom Hat Company and chances are they can rehabilitate it. The office scrapbook shows numerous before and after pictures of hats that have come in as wrecks and gone out looking like an old cowboy after a winter at the V.A. hospital at Fort Harrison. Miraculously reconstituted, that is to say. For $26, the Kirkpatricks do a clean and block that puts new life in the old sombreros.

Any buckaroo, buckarette, Swiss yodeler or teddy bear that needs a new hat can get it at the Kirkpatrick Hat shop, but they'll have a wait. About four months, as of early 1994.

The Kirkpatrick hats come with a guarantee, which has not had much use so far. "We replaced one that a horse stepped in," Sheila said. "That's the only complaint we've had."

Glenn Swank

DANIEL N. VICHOREK

Glenn Swank with his Mexican saddle.

A choice of careers was never a big issue with Glenn Swank. He was born in Hardin and went to school when he could, but the open range called him early. Glenn's father was a cowpuncher, and Glenn started drawing checks in the same line of work when he was thirteen.

From the time of his birth he lived with his family at various camps on the Dana ranch, one of the really big spreads located partly on the Crow Reservation. Glenn couldn't guess at the acreage, but noted that just the Montana part of the ranch was forty or fifty miles wide.

The family usually moved closer to town in the winter so Glenn could go to school, but Glenn's school year tended to start a little late in the fall, after the fall roundup, and he shortened the term in the spring by pulling out of school about the time the roundup wagon pulled out for the range. The roundup wagon offered an education more to his liking, he said. The wagon boss would stake him a couple of gentle horses, and they let him sleep in the nighthawk's bed. The nighthawk herded the horses at night and slept during the day.

The men on the roundup wagon liked him, Glenn said, and they showed him the cowboy trade. He said he was a lot better student of cowboy science than he was at his regular school. "I watched those old cowboys to see how they did things, and I took pride in doing things right." These days, he said, young ranch hands don't pay any attention to more experienced men. "They don't know if cows roost in trees or sleep sideways."

Glenn's academic career ended when he didn't get around to enrolling in the seventh grade. "I'd been raised by all those old punchers and by that time the teacher and the other kids didn't speak my language."

After leaving school he went on the payroll for E.L. Dana. He drew the same wage as the experienced hands—$40 a month—top money in ranch country at the time. He didn't have to worry about what to do with this bonanza because his mother collected his checks. He never saw them at all, and said he was proud to contribute to his family.

In his first years with the Dana ranch, Glenn said, a major portion of the work was trailing cattle between different parts of the ranch. The Montana portion of the ranch was west of the Bighorn River just north of the Bighorns and Pryors and the Wyoming portion was near Parkman, a distance of about seventy-five miles. The cowboys took the cows over to Parkman in the fall, usually in three bunches of about 800 each. The roundup wagon and eight or ten men went along on the trip with each bunch, which usually took about three days, Glenn said.

Coming back in the spring took longer because the cows would have new calves with them. Besides the three bunches of cows, the cowboys brought back about 1,500 to 2,000 head of yearling heifers, calves from the previous year.

The spring drives were complicated by the Bighorn River, which would be in flood in late May and June, and difficult to cross. Two crews attended the crossing, one on each side. The crew with the cattle cut willow switches and drove the cattle into the water, swimming their horses when necessary and smacking the cattle with the willow switches. Glenn said crossing one herd could take three days. Some of the cattle would turn back to the side they came from, and have to be rounded up and driven back into the water. The second crew gathered the cattle when they made it across and took them to the summer range, while the first crew and the wagon turned back to the Wyoming ranch to get another bunch.

The Dana ranch was sold in 1937, with all 32,000 head of its cattle. In the following years, Swank worked for other ranches, but always in the same job description: "strictly a cowpuncher." In those years of the mid- to late 1930s, the cowboy life on the big ranches was much the

MICHAEL S. CRUMMETT

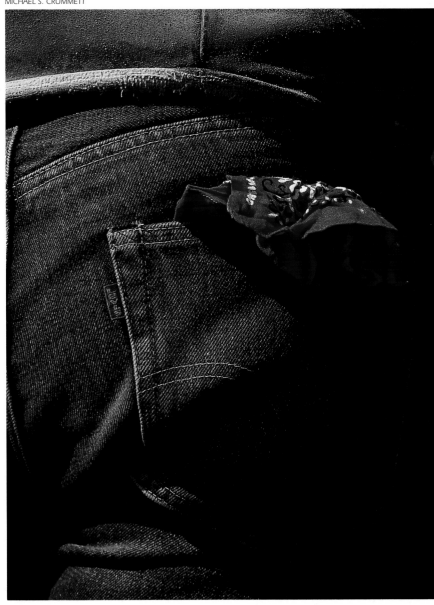

MICHAEL S. CRUMMETT

WAYNE MUMFORD

Left: Time out for the camera.

Facing page, clockwise from left:
Water filter, air filter, tourniquet, sling, horse hobble, you name it—the "plain old" bandanna.
Unloading the cookstove at branding.
Tack shed on the historic Grant-Kohrs ranch.

The nighthawk herded the horses around all night and brought them in at 4 A.M. The wagon boss always kept a horse picketed and saddled in case the nighthawk somehow lost the horse herd.

same as it had been since the turn of the century. Fences were still scarce, cattle ran on the open range, cowboys were strictly horsemen, and the roundup wagon spent a six-month tour on the range with the cattle.

"Sixteen hour days were not uncommon," Swank said. Breakfast was at 4 A.M., dinner at 10, supper at 4 P.M. "Normally you changed horses after each meal," he said. At 8 P.M. the men caught and picketed their night horses; each man normally stood guard over the cattle for two hours each night, the watches running in two-hour increments from 8 P.M. to 4 A.M. Two men stood guard at a time. The nighthawk herded the horses around all night and brought them in at 4 A.M. The wagon boss always kept a horse picketed and saddled in case the nighthawk somehow lost the horse herd, Glenn said.

In those days, Glenn said, cowboying was not usually a year-round occupation. When he was twenty, Glenn started taking summers off from ranch work and working the professional rodeo circuit. He started riding in amateur rodeos when he was sixteen, and spent sixteen years on the professional circuit. He didn't rope calves or bulldog steers in the rodeo, but was strictly a "rough stock" rider: bulls and bucking horses. He also entered wild horse races. Rodeo critters gave him a few close calls, he said. He got hooked by a few bulls, and hung up in his rigging and dragged by horses a few times, but took no major casualties beyond a broken collar bone. "I made a little better than a living at it," he said.

When he wasn't rodeoing, Glenn was working on ranches as a regular cowboy, summer and winter. A lot of guys were laid off in the winter, he said, and hung around town, shacked up with girls, or drifted back to the ranch when their money was gone and loafed until spring. One old cowboy told Glenn there was no better place for a cowboy to winter than Montana. All you had to do was get a hotel room and enough meal tickets to last until spring and you were set. You could sit in the lobby of the hotel

and put your feet up on the steam register. This was a lot better than crawling up into a frozen saddle, Glenn said, but he didn't know if any cowboy ever spent a sensible winter sitting in a warm hotel.

Glenn didn't spend his winters in hotel lobbies. He lived in the "line shacks" strung at long intervals across the range, and crawled into the frozen saddle every day all winter to check the cattle. He rode from shack to shack with his bed tied on a horse. Frostbite was a common companion, despite heavy clothing. Glenn said in cold weather he wore long underwear, Levis, a wool shirt, blanket-lined Carhartt "sourdough pants" over the Levis, a Scotch cap, big muffler, and cloth overshoes. He had to chop water holes open and keep a sharp eye out for cattle that were lousy or not wintering well. These he would take to where they could be deloused or fed.

In the summertime at the Dana ranch, most of the cowboys usually got laid off for a couple of weeks after moving the cattle to summer pasture. Glenn said this layoff was a sort of vacation for them. "They spent their vacations with whiskey and women."

After the layoff came branding, which could take a month at the Dana ranch. Then there was another layoff for a couple of weeks. After that it was time to gather up the dry cows (cows not producing calves) to be trailed to the railroad and shipped. After that, lasting into October, it was time to round up the beef steers for shipment. After the steers were shipped, it was time to drive the cows to the home ranch in Wyoming. When all the cattle that were sold had been shipped and the others lodged safely on the winter range, the roundup wagon could proceed to the home ranch and the cowboys be laid off. Often this would be about Christmas, Glenn said. During the whole time the wagon was on the range each year, six months or so, the cowboys would not once sit on a chair or at a table, Glenn said.

In the spring, most of the same cowboys would be

back to resume the strenuous life of a cowboy on the same ranch. "There was a great loyalty in those days," Glenn said, "and it cut both ways." Cowboys were loyal to their boss and proud of their outfit, and the bosses took care of the cowboys. When a man got too old for regular cowboy work, the ranch where he had spent his years would keep him around to feed hay to bulls and horses, or whatever he could do. His medical bills were paid, and so was his funeral.

It was a great life for a SINGLE MAN, HE said, but somewhat lacking for a married man. Glenn got married when he was twenty. "I was gone for a month at a time," he said. In the years that he worked on the ranches, his wife visited him only once, he said. Nevertheless, their family expanded, eventually totaling four daughters and a son. "We all grew up together," he said.

In 1958, Glenn got into the ranching business for himself, with a little spread in the Wolf Mountains east of Hardin. He and his wife brought up their family and lived the life of small ranchers for many years, well into the 1980s. They raised sheep and cattle.

Glenn was seventy-two when I visited him and his family had long since grown up, of course. Now he lives alone in his trailer in Pryor, except when he's out riding for somebody. He's been spending his summers working on a cattle and sheep ranch near Sand Springs. I visited him in Pryor just as he was about to lay off for the winter, and asked him about his days as a young cowboy. What he told me is what I have written above.

He has a saddle that he is proud of, Mexican-style with a horn big enough to set a small TV on. He doesn't ride that one much any more; "Ever since I became pear-shaped, I've had a tendency to go off over the front of it," he said.

I asked him about other cowboy equipment, and what he wore when he was a top hand. I asked him specifically about hats. "They used to say that cowpunchers wore a size two-and-a-half hat," he said, "and put a lamp wick under the band to take up the extra space." Seriously, though, the boys wore John B. Stetsons, with a few Dobbs in the later years. Each model of Stetson had a name like "Trail Boss," or "Roughrider." Glenn wore a Trail Boss.

Boots were mostly made to order for each man, usually of kangaroo or French calf leather. Saddles were from D.E. Walker, or N. Porter, or Coggeshell in Miles City or Connally in Billings, and cost anywhere from $85 to $120.

I asked Glenn how he keeps himself entertained during the long winters between riding jobs. He held up some video tapes. "Professional wrestling!" he said. "Some people say it's phony, but there's nothin' phony when they're fightin' for those buckles. They bang their heads on posts and stairs, hit 'em with chairs; some of them are dirty crooked cheatin's SOBs."

Glenn said he has only one regret about his life as a cowboy. "If I had her to do over I'd do her the same but I'd drink less," he said. He said he hasn't taken a drink for thirty-three years.

MICHAEL S. CRUMMETT

MICHAEL S. CRUMMETT

Above: Relaxing at the Bronze Bull in Billings.
Right: Virgil James roping on the Grapevine Ranch.
Far right: A fight breaks out on the picket line.

Facing page: Cook Clarence Scobey sits back while the branding crew samples his work on the Padlock Ranch.
MICHAEL S. CRUMMETT

BOB ZELLAR/J-R AGENCY

Benny Reynolds

Benny Reynolds in winter
plumage.

DANIEL N. VICHOREK

Every profession has its dean, and the dean of Montana rodeo is Benny Reynolds. In his latter fifties now, Reynolds still competes on the senior circuit, or did until an ornery critter put him into a neck brace in 1993.

When I visited him at his ranch near Twin Bridges in 1994, he was still wearing the neck brace and looking a little like Quasimodo. The living room walls of Reynolds' ranch house are covered with the many awards he has won, and photographs of himself seemingly instants away from being obliterated by fierce and enormous beasts on the rampage.

In my travels for this book, many people told me I should talk to Reynolds, but I was reluctant because Reynolds is famous as a man of few words. The word he's most famous for is "Yup." More on that later.

As a boy, Benny told me, he lived on the family ranch near Melrose. Two brothers liked to ride bucking horses, and Benny followed them. He started getting on bucking horses in 1948 or 1949 when he was twelve or thirteen years old. He practiced other events too, started going around to rodeos, and in 1960 he finished the National Finals Rodeo as the Champion Bareback Rider. The next year, he was the Champion All-Around Cowboy.

I asked him if he ever got scared. "I never did get done bein' scared," he said. "It affects everybody differently," he said. In his case, fear gave way to concentration. "You get real quiet," he said. "You know you can win if everything goes right, if the horse doesn't stumble, if you don't break the barrier, and a lot of other things that can go wrong that you have no control over."

The rodeo audience has no effect on him, he said. "You don't even know they are there. Sometimes it spooks a horse, though."

When he was young, Reynolds said, he liked rodeo a lot better than he liked school. "Nothin' in school interested me," he said, though he did finish high school.

Later, traveling with the rodeo provided many educational experiences. Traveling as far as Edmonton and Hawaii, Reynolds said, was a real thrill for a small-town boy. His first time in New York City, he recalled, "I walked up to the top of her head. The old gal there. Statue of Liberty. Walked up to her head and looked out over the town. And I got to see the boat. The old boat. The *Mayflower* that the pilgrims came on. And it was interestin', thinkin' about people comin' across the ocean on that boat."

New York in 1958 was the scene of one of Reynolds' most famous performances. A quiz show called *Name that Tune* was looking for gimmicks and somebody thought a Montana cowboy would help spice the show up. There was no rodeo performance on Monday, which was the day of the show, so they called Benny up. He said he was paired up with a young woman who was "an exchange student from New England," and luckily, he said, she knew a lot of songs. The show featured two-person teams who tried to be the first to recognize and say the name of songs that were played. Reynolds and his partner won, and came back the next week to defend their title.

The first week, they asked him questions on the show and he tried to answer "yes," but it always came out "yup," he told me. The producers of the show loved this, and the next week they rigged it up so all the questions could be answered yes or no, or yup or nope. Millions of people saw the show, and Montana's cowboy image got another boost.

Eventually, Reynolds and his wife bought their own ranch, partly with his rodeo earnings. They have a son, Rooster, who performs at rodeos. Reynolds said he tried to persuade Rooster to stay off the bulls and bucking horses, but he wouldn't listen. Finally, Reynolds said, "A bull persuaded him. Tore most of his clothes off." So now the younger Reynolds stays off the rough stock. Rooster also teaches classes in rodeo skills.

Reynolds said that steer roping is getting more popular, along with combinations of roping with other sports. One example is "rope and stroke," where teams rope steers and then golf for a total score.

"I'm no good at golfin'," Reynolds said, although he said he practices hitting the ball out in his hayfield. "I don't ski either," he said, referring to the latest thing, "rope and ski."

Among the recent highlights of his life, Reynolds said, was helping out with the sequel to the movie *Lonesome Dove*. "It was phonier than hell," he said. He said he thought the heroes should ride their own bucking horses if they wanted to be heroes, rather than have stunt men to do it.

Regarding the future of the cowboy life, Reynolds said environmentalists might succeed in shutting down rodeos, but there will always be cowboys because there will always be cows, and you can't take 'em up to the forest with a motor sickle.

I asked Reynolds who the real cowboys are these days. "It's gettin' hard to tell," he said. "Everybody's got a hat and boots. But it ain't what you wear. You could wear an ear ring or a nose ring or a baseball hat and still be a cowboy."

I asked him if he sees any difference in the way outsiders regard cowboys now, compared to his earlier days. He said cowboys have always been famous. "I guess we got famous savin' people from the Indians."

"I never did get done bein' scared."

BERT GILDART

MICHAEL S. CRUMMETT

Above: Roping on the Hibbard ranch outside of Cascade.
Right: Bedding down their saddles for the night.

A Rodeo Cowboy's Bad Day

When a rodeo cowboy has a bad day, it really is a bad day. Shawn Davis, World Champion Saddle-Bronc Rider in 1965, 1967, and 1968, had a dandy bad day in 1969. That was the day when a horse bucked him off at a rodeo in Thompson Falls and crushed his spine. An ambulance, one of which always stands by during these formal cowboy fun-fests, came rolling officially into the arena dust where Davis reposed. The ambulance attendants checked Davis out. He was alive anyway, so they gave him plenty of painkiller and loaded him into the ambulance for the trip to Missoula. Things should have gotten better for Davis then, but his bad luck continued when the ambulance attendants slammed the door on one of his hands, smashing his fingers. On the way to Missoula, the ambulance ran out of gas.

Despite this emergency medical care, Davis made a comeback on the rodeo circuit. One year and one month later, after spinal fusion surgery and six months in a body cast, he returned to rodeo competition, and in the following years was frequently near the top, although he never was champion again. Today he is head of the horse department at the College of Southern Idaho, and coach of the rodeo team. (From *Moments in Rodeo*, by Ernest Tooke.)

One cowboy"s not-so-good day at Miles City.

LARRY MAYER/BILLINGS GAZETTE

Jim Salmond and the Cattle Queen of Montana

Elizabeth Collins (date unknown).

E.R. SHEPARD PHOTO, MONTANA HISTORICAL SOCIETY

Entertainment mavens suggest that *Cattle Queen of Montana* was one of the worst movies Ronald Reagan ever made. If true, this is unfortunate, for the Queen herself, Libby Collins, certainly deserved better treatment. Merely being portrayed by Barbara Stanwyck was not enough.

Libraries in Montana have at least two of the very few known copies of Mrs. Collins' life story, *The Cattle Queen of Montana*, the title page of which promises "Narratives of thrilling adventures, recitals of stirring events, tales of hardships and privations…" and much more.

At the time of her writing, Mrs. Collins was comfortably ensconced at her ranch near Choteau, in which vicinity she was the first white woman to take up residence, with her daughter the first white child born there. The ranch today is owned and operated by Mrs. Collins' great grandson, Jim Salmond, and his sons. Though beset by hurricane-force winds, this land is coveted by tycoons and celebrities that I shall name later.

Mrs. Collins was born Elizabeth M. Smith at Rockford, Illinois in 1844, and moved with her parents ten years later to the territory that later became Iowa. Shortly thereafter she went with her parents to Colorado, her father having apparently been infected by the gold bug. With no luck mining in Colorado, Libby and her father went to New Mexico, having heard reports of rich gold finds there. Finding no gold there, they returned to Denver.

One stirring event that she recited regarding their time in New Mexico had to do with a man attacked by a jaguar. Libby was close at hand and grabbed the man's revolver after he dropped it. Like a true frontier heroine, she cut loose at the jaguar, but instead wounded the man in the thigh. Her next shot was better, and killed the big cat.

Libby had one of her "anecdotes of personal experience" in Denver when she was wounded by a stray bullet that came from a gambling tent. On another occasion, she was shot in the kneecap while she and her brother were running from Indians.

Soon after her return to Denver, her father died, and she went into the freighting business with her brothers. During this time she was captured by Indians, then rescued by cavalry after many thrilling adventures.

In the early 1860s, the freighting business brought her up the Bozeman Trail to Virginia City, Montana, where she further developed her life-long enthusiasm for mining. The brother who had come with her returned to Denver, leaving her on her own. She went to Helena, where she took up nursing as a profession. While tending a dying woman, she saw a red glow and heard a commotion that indicated that Helena was having one of the frequent fires it had in those years. The fire consumed all of Libby's worldly goods.

A party of eighteen miners at Canyon Creek northwest of Helena hired her to cook for them at $75 a month, partly because they wanted to help her out and partly because they really needed a cook. On New Year's Eve, 1874, she married Nat Collins, "whom I had been acquainted with for about two years." Collins had a placer mine at Silver City, not far from Helena. Family tradition holds that Collins was a Vigilante in the earlier days, and his cattle brand, "77," was derived from the Vigilante code, 3-7-77. The Salmond ranch still uses this brand today.

Collins' mine produced fairly well and the newlyweds were happy at Silver City for a while, but then they hit a run of bad luck. Mr. Collins broke his leg badly in an accident with a horse, and Libby shattered her ankle immediately afterward when she went to get water for him. The two of them spent some months in the hospital and returned with their bag of gold poorer by $1,500, equivalent to about $27,000 at 1993 gold prices.

Back on their claim after their hospital stay, they

had just enough time to eat supper before a sudden flood washed out their reservoir and nearly a mile of sluice boxes. They decided to give up mining and go into the livestock business. With 180 head of cattle, they settled into a rented ranch in the Prickly Pear (Helena) Valley, only to sustain heavy winter losses to their livestock the next two years.

Nat Collins began casting about for a better location and, hearing good things about the Teton Valley, went and took a look. He liked what he saw, and the Collinses drove their remaining stock to the Old Agency on the Teton where they headquartered their operation about a half mile from the future site of Choteau. Their only child, Carrie, was born November 24, 1881.

Mrs. Collins wrote that life was lonely the first few years in the Teton. She didn't see another white woman for over a year after they settled there, and the next one that came was the only one for some time. Their only neighbors and associates were Indians, and though these "were very kind and obliging and the best of neighbors," she still longed to see another white woman.

Time went by, the occasional new settler began to show up, and the Collinses' herd grew. Presently the population of settlers was so great that a physician took up residence. The Methodist preacher W.W. Van Orsdel occasionally dropped by to preach, and soon the Collinses "felt that indeed we were a favored people and that soon we would be in the midst of civilization."

This civilization came on apace, and by 1886 the Collinses were obliged to look for a roomier location for their expanded cattle operation. They moved twenty-five miles to the west, to Willow Creek near the foot of Ear Mountain, and there they again prospered. Libby Collins was not yet "The Cattle Queen of Montana," but the time was near at hand.

Sometime in the 1880s, mining fever again got hold of Mrs. Collins, as it occasionally had before. Earlier, one

Facing page: Open-range branding at a 1907 roundup.

of her brothers had found what appeared to be good mining prospects at the head of Lake McDonald in what later became Glacier National Park. These prospects were so promising, she wrote, that she hired a crew of eighteen men to develop the site, with herself as cook and boss. They worked three summers and a winter until the vein finally pinched out. Despite considerable outlay for no gain, she pronounced herself adequately compensated by the scenery.

Up until 1890, the Collinses followed the local custom of selling their cattle to buyers that came around to the ranch. Mrs. Collins developed the idea that they were not receiving full value, and nagged her husband into finally sending a consignment to Chicago. They got a better price, and the following year, just before they were going to ship, Nat Collins' already poor health took a downturn and he could not make the trip. Somebody had to accompany the cattle, and Libby decided it should be she.

This was the Victorian age and, as Mrs. Collins wrote, a woman traveling with cattle "was an event as yet unheard of in the cattle industry." Somehow, the railroad had conceived of such a possibility and passed a specific rule against it. The rule prohibited the granting of a pass to any woman who wished to accompany stock upon a cattle train, and forbade her even to ride upon such a train if she paid full fare. Confronted with these barriers when she tried to load her cattle on the train in Great Falls, Mrs. Collins went down by the river and had a good cry. She said it was the second cry of her adult life, the first being when her brother left her and returned to Denver.

She then rose up with new resolve, went into town where she met a bigwig from Chicago, and asked him to telegraph the railroad for permission to travel with her stock. The pass was immediately granted, along with a notice to conductors and employees on the train to make

Waiting for the wind to end is not a very profitable use of time in this area.

her comfortable, and warning that they would be fired if they did not.

As the train was about to pull out, Mrs. Collins went up the steps into the caboose where she was to ride, and a group of cowboys and ranchmen on the station platform waved their sombreros and sent up a cheer for "The Cattle Queen of Montana." The title stuck. Her husband remaining in poor health, she made many more trips to Chicago in following years, always with success. Newspapers chronicled her odd penchant for doing a man's job, and reassured readers, "There is nothing masculine in her appearance or conversation," and that her home was beautifully furnished.

When she wrote her book near the end of her life, Mrs. Collins gave quite a lot of space to cowboys. As an explanation to outsiders, she wrote that there were no farms in Montana, only ranches, and that the common laborers were called cow-boys and their horses were cow-horses.

The cowboy life, she said, was far from easy. "Arising with the early morning they went hurrying hither and thither far away across the open prairie, about the foothills, up the mountain side and through the valleys searching for stock."

Cowboys were "bright, active, intelligent young men, generous, liberal to a fault, and…possessed of many noble qualities," she wrote. She added that although a few of them were worthless, the average was "fair-minded, noble-hearted, generous, and a whole-souled man." And also, "true types of manly courage, generosity and activity."

Mrs. Collins took good care of her cowboys. "Many are the poor boys whose broken bones or limbs I have bandaged as they lay upon the rocks or hard dry earth of the prairie…where they had been injured by a vicious horse or enraged animal." The cowboys called her "Aunty," and sometimes "Mother." The world might call her "cranky," she said, or "rough and uncouth," but she

would rather be known as the cowboys' Aunty or Mother than to sit upon a throne as royalty.

As the 1890s wore on, the country around Choteau was more and more taken up by settlers, and the ranches of the open range were seriously pinched for room. In the first years that the Collinses were on Willow Creek, their cattle ranged as much as 100 miles away and were not likely to be seen until gathered up during the roundup. The Collinses apparently made themselves a nice fortune while the open range lasted, but when it started to close up, Mrs. Collins got restless. Civilization became too much of a good thing.

As she wrote, "I was tiring of the quiet life I was forced to lead." Rumors of gold strikes were drifting around, and soon "I felt the desire for excitement burn in my blood and I could not resist." There was only one thing that could be done: "I started for the golden land by the way of Seattle, and on the first day of a sunny July," was at Nome, Alaska, a city of 16,000 white tents containing 40,000 people. Prices were high and accommodations sparse, she reported. Gold was there in plenty, visible in the sand and even in the grass roots, but there was no water to wash it out. Before the long the excitement ceased to burn in her blood and she headed home, the prospect of which she appreciated that much more after getting a serious dose of seasickness aboard the ship. "From this time on," she said, "I have lived an uneventful life."

After her return, she was mainly given to the care of her husband, who remained sickly and died three years later. The Montana winters got too tough for her in her later years, and she did what a lot of Montanans have done since: spent them in California.

Long before Mrs. Collins died in 1921, she had a sense that the opportunities for ranching were greatly diminished. Her once extensive ranch, she said, was "remodeled into two hay farms," surely a comedown for the Cattle Queen of Montana. However, as commonly happens, the wheel of change that afflicts one generation keeps on grinding around to benefit those that follow.

One of the settlers that came to the mountain front on Willow Creek and helped pinch off the grazing available to the Collinses was a man named Frank Salmond. He arrived in Montana in 1890. In 1904, he married twenty-three-year old Carrie Collins, daughter of Nat and Libby, who lived across Willow Creek a mile or so to the north.

The Salmonds lived on their place for more than forty years, but it remained for their son, John C., to build the place into a major cattle ranch. This was possible primarily because the homesteaders who had filled up the country starting in the 1890s went broke and left. The history could be told in lights. Before 1886, the velvet darkness along the mountain front was broken only by the campfires of Indians or the occasional trapper or prospector. Gradually, as more people came, the night was speckled with the lights of homesteads over all the land. In the 1930s, almost all of the lights went out at once when the homesteaders loaded their sparse possessions on their wagons and cleared out. Much of the land that had grazed the Collins herds fifty years earlier could be purchased cheap, sometimes for as little as 10¢ to the acre. Cattle were cheap too; down to 3.5¢ a pound for prime steers, but Salmond managed to expand the ranch to 40,000 acres with 1,200 head of cattle.

This is the ranch operated today by Jim Salmond, son of John C., and Jim's sons. I asked Jim if there were any cowboy activities that I could observe on his ranch, and he invited me out to witness the fall shipping of calves. As I drove out from Choteau on the appointed day, it was apparent that the weather was not going to be ideal. Specifically, the famous Choteau wind was whipping up in puffs that rocked my pickup and blasted sand into my windshield.

Waiting for the wind to end is not a very profitable use of time in this area, though, so I wasn't surprised to find that activities were well under way when I arrived at the Salmond ranch not long after daylight. Jim's sons and some helpful neighbors were on foot in the corrals, separating different bunches of cattle and chasing them into different pens according to their status. I sat with Jim in his pickup and helped him supervise. Other superintendents included the buyer of the cattle, the banker, and the brand inspector. The remaining important participants were the truck drivers who would haul off the calves. The drivers and the trucks were supposed to be there but they weren't, and nobody knew where they were. The cattle buyer fumed and made telephone calls, trying to find out about the trucks. Presently another of Salmond's neighbors came to help and reported that the trucks were stranded along the road between Choteau and the ranch, the drivers afraid to move them because the wind was too strong. They sent along word that they weren't going to move until the wind went down, which didn't seem a good bet since it was still gaining strength. The neighbor reported a wind reading of 100 m.p.h. AT his place. Jim said he didn't think it was hardly more than 60 m.p.h. where we were, but getting stronger.

With the early arrival of the trucks in doubt, Jim took me on a tour around the ranch. I had to be careful getting out of the truck to take pictures or to open gates because the wind was strong enough to turn a pickup door into a kite if you opened it in the wrong direction.

As we moved toward the mountain front, I became puzzled by something that appeared to be a plume of smoke or steam coming up out of a draw. "Wind is blowing the reservoir away," Jim said by way of explanation. We soon arrived at the source of the plume and saw that in fact a little reservoir not more than 100 yards long was covered with raging whitecaps. Breakers were crashing into the rock-fill dam at the lower end and

MICHAEL S. CRUMMETT

the water that splashed was picked up as a heavy spray and smashed into the downwind hillside. Any person on that hillside would have been instantly soaked, if not also knocked flat by the blast. Jim said it was not uncommon for some of the other reservoirs on the ranch to be completely dried up by the wind.

Just above the reservoir at the edge of a hayfield there was a little patch of wild rose bushes. Salmond told me that was the only remainder of the original home occupied by Nat and Libby Collins. On the hillside just above the building site is a pit, all that is left of a mining attempt by the Collinses. Salmond said they were convinced that the veins of copper found in Butte ran north, and they hoped to find the other end of them.

Off to the southwest a mile or so, the old cabin where J.C. Salmond was born in 1907 still sits on the flat above Willow Creek. In some nearby aspen groves at the foot of the mountain is evidence of another phase of Montana history. Pits and low spots in the ground, barely visible and with sizable aspens growing out of them, are all that is left of an Indian village that existed there from about 1880 until 1940.

These were mixed-blood Cree Indians, known as Métis, WHO FLED to Montana from Canada after the Riel Rebellion, a major event in western Canadian history. The charismatic and erratic leader of the rebellion, Louis Riel, taught school at St. Peter's Mission near Sun River in 1883 and 1884.

In 1884, some of Riel's close associates from the Rebellion in Manitoba in the '60s came and asked him for help in what turned out to be the Riel Rebellion, Part II, this time in Saskatchewan. Leaving Fort Benton on the way north, Riel pointed at some nearby high ground and told a priest who had accompanied him that far: "I see a gallows on top of that hill, and I am swinging from it." This turned out to be an accurate vision of the fate that awaited Riel in Canada.

As a result of the Riel rebellions, many of the Métis took up temporary or permanent residence in Montana. Several small villages were established along the Rocky Mountain front, including the one at Willow Creek.

"They could have owned the whole country if they had homesteaded," Jim Salmond told me. But that was not their way. The original Métis and their descendants built cabins and a long house on Willow Creek and lived as well as they could.

One means of their survival was working on the Salmond Ranch. Jim said a difference between the Salmond ranch and others was the work force of Indians that was readily available whenever needed. They were good workers, he said, with only one shortcoming. That was a tendency to disappear instantly whenever a stranger came around.

"They'd be out in the field working with horses and a stranger would show up and the next thing you knew the horses were still out there but the Indians were gone. They never got over their fear of being forcefully returned to Canada, as happened to some Métis. Jim said Canadian Mounties assisted by U.S. Cavalry led a group of Métis back to Canada in the time of the second Riel Rebellion. Besides working on the Salmond ranch, the Métis made a little money doing other things, such as selling firewood in Choteau. By the early 1940s, most of the originals who were afraid of the Canadians had died, and the new generation left the villages at the foot of the mountains for the wider society, where they remain.

Jim said the hay harvest on the Salmond ranch was once a major operation, requiring a hundred teams of horses and forty men. Now, the same work is done by Salmond's three sons and their wives, with power equipment.

The Indians are gone, but something of the frontier still remains in the life at the Salmond Ranch. For example, there are grizzly bears. "One year," Jim said, "a

Jim Leachman and his crew, near Billings.

grizzly dug up my garden and ate all my carrots and potatoes. He didn't bother the onions. As he left, he smashed our garbage container. I guess he was mad." When they saw the wreckage the next day, Jim said, "We wondered if it was somebody from outer space. Then we saw the bear tracks."

DANIEL N. VICHOREK

Jim Salmond.

Salmond's sons, whom he describes as "two cowboys and a mechanic," may be the last Salmonds to work on the historic ranch. Jim said that although the ranch has never been up for sale, he continues to get offers of big money for the place. Ted Turner wanted it, the Church Universal and Triumphant wanted it, the Nature Conservancy wanted it, and most recently, Ross Perot wanted it. Most of these aspirants did not want to raise cattle. They want it because it is one of the most beautiful places in Montana, right up against the mountains with fourteen miles of boundary along U.S. Forest Service land.

A day or so after Ross Perot was in Helena during the 1992 political campaign, Jim saw a Lear jet flying along the mountains over his ranch. Shortly after, a Perot man called and offered him $20 million for the place. He turned that down, but Perot then offered him $30 million. The trouble is, he said, he'd have to find another ranch to buy for $30 million, and ranches like that are hard to find. The old ranch provides a good living for his family, he said, and his sons like living there. If it weren't for his sons, he said,

he'd take the money and run. He said the only problem with the old ranch is the wind, which sometimes blows fifty miles an hour for a month at a time. All the buildings at the ranch are low to the ground and the windows have shutters on the upwind side. Dealing with the wind gets old, he said.

"I used to ask why in the world they put the buildings out here on the prairie when they could have put them closer to the mountain and got less wind. It was because of the Indians. The brush was full of Indians and they wanted to stay some distance from them."

For her part, the Cattle Queen didn't seem to mind the wind. She never mentions it directly in her book, but in her closing line, she said that even though her ranch was no longer what it had been, "yet I seem to breathe more fully there the free air of the plains...."

Index

Rodeo grand entry, Billings.